Gaslighting Recovery
Workbook 2022

Effective Tips and Strategies for Holistic Healing from Emotional Abuse

Table of Contents

Introduction

Gaslighting Recovery Workbook sheds light on the basics of emotional abuse. This book explores questions like: "What is emotional abuse? "What does gaslighting mean and how do I identify a gaslighter? and "How do I heal from a toxic relationship? It further looks into the effects of abuse and manipulation on your life. If you believe you are the victim of a gaslighter, this book is for you.

Part one of the book focuses on understanding the gaslighter. It discusses the concepts of emotional abuse and toxic behavior in depth. It also explores gaslighting in detail, including what the term means, how it originated and how you can recognize it. It looks at the signs, traits, and behaviors that can help you identify whether someone is a gaslighter.

This book also explains what narcissism is and how it is related to gaslighting. Gaslighting Recovery Workbook discusses how a gaslighter does not always have to be a narcissist, but a narcissist will always be a gaslighter. Narcissists are self-serving, insecure, and extremely manipulative individuals who will do anything to get things their way. They have no regard for other people and will use and abuse them for their own benefit. This book goes into detail to discuss the consequences of manipulation and gaslighting and the grave effects it has on the victim. The victim of abuse goes through mental and physical anguish that is not always visible. This is why it is important to recognize the signs and get yourself out of the toxic situation as soon as possible.

Gaslighting Recovery Workbook looks at how you can exit your toxic relationship. It requires a lot of courage to leave an abusive relationship. Even though it is extremely difficult to escape the clutches of a narcissist, it is not impossible. This book focuses on how you can heal yourself. It explains how, to start healing, you will need to focus and take some time out to understand what gaslighting is and what happened in the relationship. This process is called the grieving process, and it is an extremely crucial part of healing. It helps you mourn the loss of your old self and the time lost. However, there is only a way forward after this.

Gaslighting Recovery Workbook then moves on to explore how you can gain confidence and rebuild your self-esteem to move forward. It stresses how important it is to work on your confidence after your gaslighter made you doubt your perception, your sense of reality, and your worth. It also focuses on the importance of establishing boundaries and healing. Creating strict boundaries helps you maintain a safe distance from your abuser is imperative for your self-esteem. This book also focuses on how you can create better relationships in the future and the importance of therapy and counseling.

Chapter 1: Toxic Behavior and Emotional Abuse

If you see someone with bruises all over their face, neck, and arms, you will probably wonder if something is wrong and you may even ask them if they are okay. You will be concerned because you can clearly see that they have been hurt. This is the case with physical abuse; it is obvious as people can see it all over your body and face. However, emotional abuse is different. Although it doesn't leave any physical marks, and you can fool your friends and loved ones into thinking that you are okay with a fake smile, it can destroy you on the inside. Soon, everyone will be able to see through your fake smile. Emotional abuse is like a monster living inside of you that feeds on your thoughts and feelings until there is nothing left of you. You will look in the mirror one day, and you won't recognize who you are anymore. This once happy and carefree person is gone and is replaced by someone you don't even know.

Since emotional abuse isn't as straightforward as physical abuse, sometimes it can be hard to understand that you are a victim. You may feel like something is wrong or that you aren't yourself, but you aren't aware that you are going through emotional abuse. Maybe you don't want to believe it because there is no way that your partner, who you are madly in love with, or your parents, who you have always idolized, can be emotionally abusive. It is hard to believe that those we love and trust the most can hurt us and manipulate us this way, but it happens more often than you think. To understand if you are a victim of emotional abuse or not, you first need to understand emotional abuse, its signs, and what it feels like.

What Is Emotional Abuse?

Emotional abuse is a tactic practiced by someone to gain control over you. They will manipulate you, embarrass you, shame you, and blame you. This won't be a one-time thing, as emotional abuse is a behavior pattern that includes degrading words and bullying. This kind of behavior is done on purpose to destroy your self-esteem and mental health. If you are terrified, confused and feel self-doubt every time you are around your partner or voicing your opinion makes you feel anxious, you are probably in an emotionally abusive relationship. That being said, emotional abuse doesn't only occur in intimate relationships and between partners.

As a matter of fact, parents, friends, grandparents, siblings, managers, and co-workers can all be emotionally abusive. They break you and isolate you to make you feel worthless and that you are nothing without them. Their only goal is to control you, to make you stay with them.

We have mentioned that it isn't always easy for a victim to be aware of experiencing emotional abuse. This is because abusers are manipulative and gaslight you into making you feel that this is all in your head or that their anger outburst is your fault. They will make you doubt yourself, and you may actually start believing that either this is all in your head or that you are the one at fault. To better understand emotional abuse, let's look at all its different types.

Gaslighting

We will start with gaslighting since it is the main topic of our book. Gaslighting is when the abuser makes you doubt yourself. They will hurt and abuse you, and when you confront them, they will deny any wrongdoing. They will tell you that you misunderstood, make you question your recollection of what happened, or that the whole incident was your fault. They may even justify the abuse by telling you that they only do this because they love you.

Verbal Abuse

Verbal abuse or name-calling is an obvious form of abuse. It is when the abuser swears at you, calls you names, and insults you. They can also make fun of your appearance, weight, or sexuality and pretend that it is all in good fun. They may even humiliate and embarrass you in front of people and disguise it as jokes. However, this is a manipulation tactic to belittle you and shake your self-esteem. Insults and name-calling aren't considered jokes, and you should never tolerate this kind of behavior.

Overprotectiveness

Overprotection can easily be disguised as your partner trying to protect you, and is seen in some cultures as a form of masculinity. There is nothing wrong when your partner is being protective or even a little jealous from time to time. It is when the protection feels over the top that it becomes a form of emotional abuse. If you feel that your partner views your relationship as more of ownership, if they see everyone you talk to as a threat, or seem aggressive towards your friends or family members, these are all red flags. If you feel that your relationships with others are being threatened and the behavior isn't normal, even if they disguise it as protection because they love you, it is still abuse. It can also be a tactic to isolate you from your loved ones. That takes us to the next point.

Isolation

You should know that an abuser wants you all for themselves; it is how they assert control. Usually, they won't isolate you all at once. They will do it gradually, so you won't suspect that something is off. They will first convince you that they are the only person that loves you and wants what is best for you and other people, whether your friends or family, want to ruin your relationship. They will then, directly or indirectly, prevent you from contacting them. In even more extreme situations, they may prevent you from living your day-to-day life like going to work or to the gym, stopping you from coming into contact with anyone else. They want to be the only person in your life, ensuring you believe their lies and manipulations. The abuser is afraid that other people will see through them and help open your eyes to their lies and manipulations. All of these controlling actions will be disguised as love.

Using Guilt

We all have boundaries, and they are essential to protect ourselves and our peace of mind. However, the abuser may use guilt, causing you to let your guard down. They will make it seem like your boundaries are hurting them or your relationship to guilt-trip you. Your boundaries are for you and your protection. They aren't hurting anyone, but your abuser will pretend that they are an issue because boundaries make it hard for them to manipulate you and abuse you.

Mind Games

Your abuser may play mind games for different reasons, like pressuring you to do something you don't want to or shifting the blame during fights. Whatever their reasons are, they will play these psychological games until they get what they want. They may even pretend that you don't exist even if you live in the same house. Basically, at times, they won't even acknowledge your presence. They may even disappear for a few days, and they won't answer any of your calls. Remember, they have already isolated you, so they are now the only person you have. That will make losing them unbearable and will make you vulnerable and ready to cave in.

Stalk You

There is no denying that stalking is very unhealthy and scary behavior. Unfortunately, it has become fairly easy to stalk people in this day and age since there is no such thing as privacy anymore. Social media has made it easy for people to know where you live and the places you frequent the most. You may be shopping at the mall or having lunch with a friend at your favorite restaurant, when you suddenly see your partner or ex-partner right in front of you. They will practice all forms of abuse like threats, guilt trips, manipulation, or gaslighting in an effort to get you back.

Sex

Sex is an act of love and passion between two consensual adults. However, abusers can use it as a method for emotional abuse. If you aren't in the mood or uncomfortable with a certain sexual act, your abusive partner may use guilt or manipulation to get you to do it anyway. You will give in to avoid punishments like the silent treatment. This can lead to serious consequences like rape or unwanted pregnancy. Remember, you aren't consenting because you want to. You are consenting out of fear or simply avoiding fights or angry outbursts.

Financial Dependence

Being financially independent can give you power, and that will make it hard for your abuser to control you. This is why they will make sure that you never have any money. They will do this by preventing you from working or limiting how much money you have at any given time. They want you to be financially dependent on them so they can have power over you and ensure you never leave them.

Controlling You

Although everything we have mentioned is mainly to assert control, some obvious controlling signs will be hard to miss. They control who you talk to, what you wear, hair color and style, and what you eat. You will basically feel like you don't have a voice and that your identity is slipping away from you.

These are all types of emotional abuse, and if you have experienced one or more of them, you are definitely the victim of it. However, an emotionally abusive individual may not act this way directly towards you. You may actually notice a pattern of behavior towards others or towards themselves as another tactic to manipulate you.

Threatening to Harm Your Pets

Everyone knows that pets are family, and they are often treated as such. However, an abuser will take advantage of the love you have for your pet to exert control over you. For instance, they may threaten to harm your pet if you ever consider leaving them and may even do so if they feel that you are determined to leave. They may also harm your pet to punish you or threaten to do so to get you to "obey" them.

Self-Harm

It goes without saying, but if anyone threatens to harm themselves to pressure you to do something, they are clearly unstable. If you notice this pattern of behavior when you tell them no or when you want to break up the relationship, this is definitely emotional abuse. They take advantage of your love for them and your good nature to garner sympathy and manipulate you.

If you are going through any of the things we have mentioned here, you need to get help immediately. You are putting your life and your pets' or children's lives in danger. An emotional abuser is a weak and unstable person who doesn't love you and can only get you to stay with them by asserting control. They have no self-esteem, and deep down, they know that they are worthless and don't deserve someone like you in their lives. Whether it is a family member, partner, friend, or co-worker who is doing this, you need to save yourself and leave. You don't deserve to live like this.

To be able to spot an abuser, you should watch out for these toxic traits or patterns of behavior.

Types of Toxic Behavior

Cheating

Cheating is a cowardly act, and it shows disrespect. If your partner constantly cheats on you, this is toxic behavior that you shouldn't tolerate. Even if they apologize and promise you that this is the last time, you should leave. It is an insincere apology, and it is never the last time. They are basically apologizing because they got caught. You don't deserve to be treated with this kind of disrespect. Additionally, cheating can destroy your self-esteem and make you feel worthless.

Playing the Victim

Some people always see themselves as victims. It is never their fault, it is always someone else's. This trait shows immaturity and an inability to take responsibility for one's actions. People who never see themselves at fault will never change. They aren't just hurting other people, but they are hurting themselves as well. If you have a parent or a partner who always plays the victim, it can be very exhausting and emotionally draining. Especially if they always shift the blame and make you the bad guy but see themselves as perfect beings who can do no wrong.

Accuses You of Overreacting

Everyone is entitled to their own feelings, and when someone doesn't give you the space to feel the things you want to feel, they are definitely toxic. For instance, if they hurt your feelings and you speak up, they will dismiss what you are saying and accuse you of overreacting. They may also belittle your feelings towards other things and show a lack of respect and compassion. If you lose a pet and are devastated, a toxic person will think you are making a big deal and belittle your feelings. This toxic behavior can come from a partner, friend, or parent. Your mom may be mad that you missed a family dinner because your dog just died and accuse you of overreacting, saying it was just an animal. A normal person understands that pets are family. Even if they don't know what you are going through exactly, they will show compassion and make you feel comfortable enough with your feelings.

Emotional Vampires

Emotional vampires are people who suck the energy out of you. They are people that make you feel emotionally drained after spending time with them. This can apply to anyone in your life. Spotting an emotional vampire isn't hard; it is a person that makes you feel worse after you interact with them. This is because these people drain your energy and exhaust you emotionally. They either spend their time complaining or talking about themselves and not giving you a chance to chime in or even ask you how you are doing.

Not Listening

Every type of relationship requires some give and take, even during conversations. You want to feel heard, to be able to vent when you feel like it, and to share stories with your loved ones. However, a toxic behavior that can frustrate many people is when you start to open up to someone about something upsetting, tell them about your day, or even share a funny story, and you notice that they are disengaged and not paying attention to you. They will then interrupt you and start talking about something else, probably themselves. This is very selfish behavior that can start to make you feel worthless because what you are saying seems unimportant or uninteresting to your partner, friend, or parent.

Not Being There for You

Imagine you lost a parent, and you are grieving and inconsolable. You need someone close to you to turn to and to provide you with emotional support. However, the one person you counted on, whether a partner, friend or relative, wasn't there for you. How would you feel? It is extremely painful when someone you have always counted on, someone you have always been there for deserts you in your time of need. They may say that they are busy, ignore your calls, and put their needs above yours.

Building Walls

Some people, for whatever reasons, build walls around themselves to keep people at a distance. They won't try to connect with you emotionally, and every time you try and get close to them, they get angry, withdraw, or try to avoid you. If you try to get them to open up and talk about their feelings, they will make jokes instead. These people aren't interested in having a real relationship with anyone. In time, you will feel disconnected, alone, frustrated, and even depressed. You certainly don't need this kind of toxicity in your life.

Toxic and abusive behavior should never be acceptable. You shouldn't let people who clearly have issues but don't want to acknowledge them ruin your life. There are always red flags at the beginning of any relationship. If you notice any of the emotional abuse signs or toxic behavior we have mentioned here, you need to take action as soon as possible. Listen to your friends or family if they think that the person you are with is no good, because they want what is best for you. They can't all be wrong, and your partner is the only one who is right. Listen to your gut feeling when it tells you to leave, even if you don't want to believe it. You may be a victim of gaslighting by a narcissist, which we will talk about in detail in the coming chapters, along with healing, recovery, and how to move on and have healthy relationships.

Chapter 2: What Is Gaslighting?

Abusive relationships come with a lot of problems. However, gaslighting has to be the worst of them all because it is often a covert and insidious form of emotional abuse. The abuse or bullying is intense in gaslighting because the victim is made to question their reality and even doubt their judgment. The victim will be under the influence and control of the abuser and would lose all sense of self and confidence. As the abuse gets more intense, the victim eventually starts to question their sanity.

This type of emotional abuse is more common in romantic relationships. However, you will also notice that it may occur among family members or friendships. People who are toxic by nature will often try to control others around them by using the manipulative power of gaslighting.

How Does Gaslighting Work?

In simple terms, gaslighting is an abusive behavioral pattern that crushes the reality perception of the victim. The victims start doubting everything around them, especially after having communicated with the abuser. The victim may feel overwhelmed and confused about everything. They often report experiencing a state of daze and uncertain if they are the ones at fault. Gaslighting is such an insidious and manipulative form of abuse that it leaves the victims feeling so hopeless that they start doubting their decisions and mental well-being.

Is It the Same as Narcissism?

Although it is not always the case, the abusers may actually have narcissistic personality disorder. Such individuals would often believe that they are the most important individual around and that everything is about them. You will find that they are quite self-absorbed and seldom show authentic interest in another person unless they need something from them. They lack empathy and the ability to comprehend what other people are going through.

Narcissists are after praise and attention. Moreover, they tend to get over-demanding and view themselves in a grandiose manner. They believe that their life and future are far more important than others around them, and they would use manipulation and cunning tactics to get what they want.

In general, narcissists have an overly inflated sense of self-significance, and they often exaggerate their success or achievements. A narcissist would go to any lengths for their own gain, and they often get angry when faced with criticism. They would always expect special treatment and would criticize others a lot. So, the victim of gaslighting gets stifled by the emotional abuse cycle and has to bear the toxic narcissistic abuse.

How to Spot Gaslighting?

The victims often get so entangled in the abusive relationship that it is hard for them to realize and acknowledge the toxicity of the relationship, let alone walk out of it. However, before you even begin to think about seeking help, it is important to understand and identify the signs of gaslighting, as they are often quite subtle and hard to spot. Victims of gaslighting often experience chronic anxiety, stress, depression, and various other mental ailments, including suicidal ideation and substance abuse. Therefore, it is imperative to spot the signs as soon as possible and seek help. Below are some ways you can identify if you or someone you know may be experiencing this type of abuse.

1. Doubting Reality and Feelings

It is common for the victims of gaslighting to experience uncertainty about the reality around them and their feelings. They will attempt to draw explanations about the situation by thinking they are overly sensitive or that their situation is not that bad. They may even trivialize their experience by saying that other people have it worse than they do.

2. Questioning Their Perception and Judgment

The victim of gaslighting may also feel scared of expressing their emotions or speaking up about their feelings. It is quite common that every time they have expressed their feelings, it creates a commotion, and they feel worse than ever. Eventually, the victim will learn to stay quiet to escape feeling bad or downtrodden. However, this will eventually crush their self-esteem, and they get tangled in this abusive relationship more and more.

3. Insecurity and Vulnerability

When the relationship is abusive with a transgressor using gaslighting to manipulate the other partner, the victim will slowly start feeling powerless. It may often feel as if they are walking on eggshells around the transgressor. The person may also suffer from low self-esteem and will often feel on edge.

4. Feeling Powerless or Alone

Over time, the victim starts believing that people around them know that the person is either unstable or strange because the abuser says so. Unfortunately, this eventually makes the victim feel isolated and powerless. The feeling of isolation is suffocating, and the victim tends to feel trapped.

5. Questioning Who They Really Are

Gaslighting is such a powerful form of emotional abuse that it causes serious damage to the victim, and they may start wondering if the gaslighter or abuser is actually right. It is unfortunate and quite heartbreaking to see victims trying to find faults within themselves and feel as if they are the ones who have been insane, inadequate, or unintelligent. The victim may often repeat or rehearse the judgmental statements in their mind.

6. Feeling of an Impending Doom

The victim often feels as if something awful will happen, and as soon as they are around the abuser, they tend to feel impending doom. This is a suffocating and sinking feeling and may involve extreme fear and anxiety. The victim may also feel threatened and constantly on edge without really understanding the reason behind it.

7. Second-Guessing Oneself

The victims of this type of emotional abuse commonly doubt themselves, their decisions, and their behavior. They may also wonder whether they can recall details of past events clearly and accurately or not. Unfortunately, the chronicity of gaslighting is so toxic and debilitating that the victim may often stop sharing anything with friends or family because they believe that whatever they may be feeling is not right.

8. Incessantly Apologizing

Interestingly and sadly enough, the victims will be so disappointed in themselves and often confused about their reality and environment that you will find them apologizing a lot. You will notice that they are often apologizing for who they are and what they may be doing.

9. Using Distraction as a Tactic

The gaslighter would also distract the victim from gaining control. If the victim asks them a direct question, the gaslighter may try hard to change the subject or confuse the victim in a lengthy or an off-track discussion, so the victim ends up feeling confused and mentally exhausted.

10.   Rewriting History

It is unfortunate that the victim in such a toxic relationship is experiencing such a manipulating form of abuse. The gaslighting not only takes an emotional toll on the victim's health but also creates situations where the abuser distorts the things that have already happened and retells them in their own way. This way, the gaslighter twists the reality of the victim to suit their needs.

The above are some classic signs that may help you identify the victim of this type of emotional abuse. If you can identify these signs in yourself or anyone around you, it is very important to seek our immediate help. The urgency of the matter cannot be stressed enough because, the longer the victim stays trapped with a gaslighter, the more powerless they feel.

Statements that Abusers Often Use

Gaslighting takes an intense toll on the overall mental well-being and self-esteem of the victim. Below are some of the most commonly used statements by abusers to exercise control over the victim. Remember that the abuser may not use the exact sentences listed below, but the context and meaning would be identical.

1. This never happened, why are you making it up?

2. Why are you always so extra sensitive?

3. You have a terribly weak memory!

4. Everyone knows how crazy you are!

5. I feel sorry that you believe that I am hurting you

6. You should have anticipated my reaction to this!

With abusers and gaslighters, the lying, exaggeration, manipulation, and fact twisting never ends because they cannot let go of the stronghold that they have on the victim.

It is worth mentioning that noticing the signs of gaslighting in a victim is just one aspect of understanding the problem. The other aspect has to deal with the transgressor and identify various stages of this abusive relationship. Below are the classical characteristics or signs that you can identify in the behavior of the abuser and note a pattern.

Stages of Gaslighting That You Need to Know

Gaslighting is as complicated as it is insidious and manipulative. However, in addition to evaluating the behavior of the sufferer or victim, it is equally important to understand the different stages involved in gaslighting. Being familiar with the stages of this abuse will help identify the problem much faster.

1. Exaggeration or Lying

Generally, the abuser will make the victim feel as if something is wrong with that person. The abuser may often blame the victim with false accusations or presumptions and will avoid being objective or providing verifiable factual accounts. It is also interesting to note that as soon as the victim mentions something factual as a counterargument or point of support, the abuser either tends to change the topic or totally cuts off the victim mid-way. A good example of exaggerating a situation is if the abuser tells the victim, "Your job is such a waste of time! I don't see what purpose it fulfills. Anyone can do this! What's so special about it?"

2. Repeating to Maintain Control

For an abuser, it is very important to maintain the stronghold in an abusive relationship. Most often, they do this by continuing manipulative behavioral tactics and using repetition. You may be wondering how repetition can be used as a control tactic, but it is quite subtle. The abuser needs to repeat the judgments or statements consistently so they stay in control of the conversation and can dominate the other person and the relationship that they share.

3. When Challenged, You See the Worst

This sounds absolutely insane, and it is more so maddening to experience because the gaslighter or the abuser will go on the offensive as soon as the victim tries to speak up. This happens when the victim tries to catch the abuser in a lie or calls them out using facts. In this situation, the gaslighter would most often make the victim feel scared or attacked by escalating the overall argument. They may also take the help of absolute denial, attacking and blaming the victim, or making more false claims to avoid any discussion.

As a result, the victim ends up feeling more overwhelmed and confused about the whole situation. They may feel shattered and exhausted from the debilitating emotional turmoil that never seems to end.

4. Burning Out the Victim

A classical tactic of a gaslighter or an abuser is to always stay on the offensive side of things because, through this manner, the gaslighter would eventually gain control. The gaslighter continues the offensive stance until the victim feels discouraged, exhausted, fearful, and the victim may end up chronically doubting themselves. Moreover, this effect lasts for a long time, and victims will be questioning and doubting their reality and identity consistently. This tactic often sounds like trivialization, and the abuser may say something like, "Right! So now you will be feeling sorry for yourself! Go ahead, feel sorry and whine."

5. Codependent Relations

Codependency is defined as excessive psychological or emotional reliance on your partner (according to the Oxford dictionary). The abuser or gaslighter will often make the victim or sufferer feel excessively anxious and insecure in the relationship. Afterward, the gaslighter has enough power to gain respect, acceptance, security, and approval of the victim. Moreover, the toxicity of this abuse does not end here. The abuser can keep threatening the victim by scaring them by taking away those things and thereby creating a poisonous codependent relationship dynamic based on vulnerability and fear.

6. The Occasional Hope!

This is yet another trick the abuser often uses to control the victim ruthlessly. Through this technique, the gaslighter would treat the victim with respect, kindness, and remorse, ultimately making the victim believe in the good that the relationship holds. The victim starts seeing a ray of hope and believes that the abuser is not a bad person and if they keep trying, things will eventually improve. However, the reality is much different because this is nothing but false hope.

7. Controlling the Victim by Domination

In an abusive relationship, the primary goal of an abuser is to gain absolute power and control their victims. It is a pathological and parasitic relationship where the victim suffers terribly because the abuser controls their life and dominates the victim. The abuser tends to gain control by taking advantage of their partner. They continue their manipulative ways and lies to keep the victims entangled in the toxic web of manipulation filled with doubt, insecurity, and chronic fear.

Once you have identified these stages or signs in a relationship, the next obvious step is to evaluate the situation and seek immediate help. Gaslighting often involves manipulative and insidious tactics, including blaming the victim, minimizing, distracting, lying, or reality distortion, and taking refuge in denial. It is difficult to survive these relationships, and without professional mental health and proper care, the victim cannot hope to win the war against this emotional abuse. It is deep-rooted in the relationship and works like a black mold that leaves its mark if left untreated and unattended.

Can There Be an Escape Plan?

The first thing that victims of abuse must understand is that dealing with any kind of abuse is never easy and often creates a lot of stress. Moreover, as soon as the victim feels overwhelmed or uncertain about how to handle the situation, they may shrink back because that seems to be the safest possible option. But this can only deflect the conflict temporarily and lets the abuser strengthen their hold over the victim. Below are some useful strategies that the victim can use to protect their well-being, sense of self and react productively.

1. It is useful to call out control and manipulation by acknowledging that it is, indeed, happening. The victim may also practice relaxation exercises to cool down.

2. Although it sounds intense, a good way to start is to let the abuser know that their behavior has a negative effect. The victim may also express their disappointment or anger politely and calmly and share how it affects them.

3. The victim needs to set clear boundaries and communicate them to the abuser. Additionally, they may state the consequence of crossing those boundaries. This is important because it allows the victim to set a safe space for themselves.

4. Understandably, the victim may end up feeling alienated from family or friends. However, they need to reach out to their trusted close ones and share to seek counsel and support.

Addressing problematic behaviors is in itself a very challenging task, and the challenge and difficulty doubles if you are dealing with an abuser. Emotional abuse happens to be one of the most malignant forms of abuse because it incapacitates the victim. However, addressing the problem vigilantly will eventually remedy the situation.

To sum it all up, it would be sufficient to say that the victim does not need to blame themselves for suffering this abuse. It is unfortunate that the victims end up feeling hopeless and will also blame themselves for all the bad things happening to them. The reality is that the gaslighter or abuser is a conscious person, and they consciously choose to torture their partner in a relationship by emotionally abusing them.

Therefore, the gaslighter or abuser is the person who should be made responsible for the toxicity and damage. However, the one thing the victim needs to do is to muster up the courage to take steps towards seeking professional and timely help. It may also be the case that the abuse or toxicity in the relationship has escalated so much that the victim needs to consider moving away or out of the relationship for the sake of their own sanity and mental well-being. It is important to prioritize your health under all circumstances and make healthy choices. As individuals, we need to be able to respect the boundaries that others set and also to be able to set healthy boundaries for ourselves.

Chapter 3: Narcissism and Gaslighting

You have probably heard the word narcissist quite a few times, from someone you know, or you were unfortunate enough to meet someone who fits the description of a narcissist. The word is derived from the Greek myth of Narcissus. He was the son of the river god, and was prophesied to live to old age provided he never knew or recognized himself. However, one day as he was drinking from a river, he saw his reflection, and he fell in love with it. He didn't want to leave or disturb the water because he didn't want to lose his reflection. Eventually, he died of thirst. Sigmund Freud was one of the people influenced by this myth, and he believed that narcissism was a part of a child's development. When we were infants, we only saw others as an extension of ourselves. Freud believed that some people never grow out of this stage, and they keep seeing others as nothing more than an extension of themselves. These people are incapable of loving anyone else but themselves, and that is what we call narcissism.

What Is Narcissism?

People have been using the word narcissism quite a lot lately. They use it to describe the behavior of some celebrities who are obsessed with their looks and take endless selfies and post them all over Instagram for attention. They are basically social media narcissists. However, from a psychological point of view, narcissism isn't only self-love or obsession with one's looks. It is when a person falls in love with an exaggerated idea or image they have of themselves. They create this image because they are insecure about who they really are and have no self-esteem. Narcissists are egotistical, extremely selfish, self-obsessed, crave admiration, and are incapable of feeling empathy. The lack of empathy makes it impossible for a narcissist to put themselves in someone else's shoes, so they will never be able to understand how others feel or sympathize with them.

Narcissism is a personality disorder that affects more men than women. People suffering from this disorder rarely seek help because they will never comprehend or feel how their behavior hurts those around them. Their huge ego makes it impossible for a narcissist to see anything wrong with them, let alone ask for help. Even if you confront them with the pain they have caused you, they will simply shift the blame and gaslight you. They don't react well to criticism because how can you or anyone criticize this perfect image that they have worked so hard to create and maintain?

To better understand narcissism, let's take a look at the different types of this disorder.

Types of Narcissism

Normal or Healthy Narcissism

You don't really expect words like normal and healthy to be in the same sentence as narcissism. However, some people can have a healthy amount of narcissism. You should also know that being narcissistic doesn't necessarily mean having a narcissistic personality disorder or NPD. A person can simply have some narcissistic traits that don't really qualify as a disorder. Some people consider a healthy amount of narcissism to be a positive thing. It is what makes us feel good about ourselves when we share our achievements with other people.

Additionally, it makes us aware of our self-worth and what we deserve. Unlike other types of narcissism, this type is rooted in reality. For instance, people with a healthy amount of narcissism won't settle for a bad relationship or a low salary because they know their worth and deserve better.

Overt Narcissism

Overt narcissism is also called grandiose narcissism, and it fits the idea that we all have of narcissists. People with overt narcissism have an unrealistic image of themselves. They feel entitled and tend to exaggerate their abilities and feel superior to other people. They basically believe that they are better than anyone, and they are experts at manipulating and controlling other people. The image they create isn't real, and it is often to hide severe insecurity.

There are two types of overt narcissism: maladaptive and adaptive. Adaptive narcissists tend to have high self-esteem, which they use as a shield to protect themselves so other people can't hurt them. They are actually very charming, attractive, and successful since they work hard to create a better version of themselves. A famous figure with a grandiose narcissism is Iron Man himself, Tony Stark. Just like Tony, they can be friendly, persuasive, and fit for leadership roles. The other type is maladaptive narcissism. These people are entitled and have no problem using others to get what they want.

Covert Narcissism

Covert narcissism is also known as vulnerable narcissism. This type is nothing like the overt type because they are neither successful nor charming. They are insecure and lack self-confidence. They crave attention, are sensitive to criticism, and deep down, they feel entitled. They desire nothing more than to be successful, but they are extremely passive and don't do anything to better themselves or their lives. Instead, they are always envious of other people's success, making them terrible friends or partners. They are very sad people who believe that no one has it worse than them. This may make you feel bad for them and want to save them. However, you can't save other people from themselves, which is why you need to set boundaries, so they don't suck you into their toxic world.

Malignant Narcissism

Malignant narcissism may be one of the most dangerous types of narcissism. These people are manipulative, aggressive, sadistic, and ill-intentioned. They don't have any feelings of guilt, compassion, remorse, or empathy and enjoy watching other people suffer. They won't think twice about exploiting the people in their lives, whether it's family or friends, to get what they want. Malignant narcissists can also be abusers since they tend to control and isolate their victims. They are often described as psychopaths or sociopaths. One of the most famous malignant narcissists is Hitler.

If someone in your life is a malignant narcissist, then you should stay away from them. Actually, you should pack your bags and run. These people are dangerous and are experts in manipulating and destroying the people in their lives. They will practice all kinds of abuse on you and won't feel any type of remorse. Confronting them will not be effective since they will gaslight you to switch blame until you start believing that everything is your fault. Gaslighting is one of the malignant narcissists' favorite weapons.

How Does Narcissism Relate to Gaslighting?

The one thing that any narcissist cares about is exerting control over their victims, and gaslighting allows them to achieve this goal. Gaslighting comes easy to a narcissist because they are skilled liars. They will make you question your sanity or make you feel that you aren't entitled to your feelings by denying certain events, accusing you of overreacting, or saying that they were just joking. You will start to question yourself and your sanity, which will take a toll on your mental health. Gaslighting is one of the narcissist's favorite tools because it gives them power over you, allows them to negate responsibility for their actions, and makes you feel guilty, all to ensure you never leave them.

Now let's take a look at how narcissism and gaslighting are related.

Nothing Is Their Fault

A narcissist gaslighter will never say that they are wrong or that something was their fault. Narcissists have low self-esteem and are very sensitive to criticism. Therefore, if you ever confront them over something they did, they will be extremely defensive and react in a very unpleasant manner. They will either deny it, get angry, make excuses, or shift blame. They can also act passive-aggressively by avoiding you, disappearing for a few days, or refusing to speak to you. These are all gaslighting tactics.

Exaggerations and Lies

Narcissism and gaslighting are basically built on exaggerations and lies. For narcissists to feel good about themselves, they must put other people down. They exaggerate everything about themselves so they can seem superior and lie to hide their insecurities. Narcissists employ gaslighting to twist the truth, destroy someone's reputation, or create a false narrative. They will continue gaslighting and lying to you even if you have proof that contradicts their story. This can be very confusing to the victim because they don't understand how they keep lying and denying what they did when they have already been caught. This isn't what normal people do. When caught in a similar situation, a person who isn't a narcissist will feel guilty and apologize for lying. However, a narcissist's behavior is anything but normal. They are toxic and thrive on the chaos, which is why gaslighting is their favorite tool for emotional torture and abuse.

Creating an Unrealistic Self Image

Narcissists have no self-esteem, are extremely insecure, and don't handle criticism well. To make up for this insecurity, they tend to create an unrealistic image of themselves. Their goal is to impress other people. When you add gaslighting to the mix, creating this perfect self-image can take a dangerous turn. In this case, a narcissistic gaslighter will destroy the people around them to feel superior. They do this by refusing to listen to you or acknowledge your feelings, or even share theirs. They will gaslight you after a fight by denying what happened or telling you that you don't remember things correctly to get you to start questioning yourself and your sanity. A narcissistic gaslighter will also make you feel that you aren't entitled to your feelings and are overreacting. They will also brainwash you by pretending that they have forgotten what happened or that you are exaggerating.

Emotional Abuse

Narcissistic gaslighters tend to cause pain and suffering to the people in their lives. This is because the only way they can feel powerful is by bringing their partners down. Their goal is to make you feel confused and insecure. They love drama and thrive on negativity, and they enjoy playing mind games and twisting the truth. They never feel any guilt, even if they see you in pain, because they simply don't care about your feelings. They may accuse you of causing them pain, and you will start believing them and may even try to make it up to them. You never know what to expect with a narcissist gaslighter since they have dangerous mood swings that can cause you extreme emotional distress.

Excellent Manipulators

We have mentioned how narcissists are excellent manipulators, and gaslighting is a great manipulation tool a few times. By employing gaslighting, a narcissist can shake your self-confidence and make you constantly question yourself. Having a conversation with them can be exhausting. This is because they see themselves as experts in any topic, so arguing with them will be futile since, from their perspective, they are the experts, and they are never wrong.

Narcissists are very dangerous individuals. They are weak creatures who pretend to be something that they aren't because of their insecurities. They cause pain and suffering to everyone in their lives, and they get high on inflicting pain. They are terrible people that should be avoided. If you have a narcissist in your life, you need to run in the opposite direction. Spotting a narcissist isn't impossible if you know what to look out for.

How to Spot a Narcissist

They Love Talking about Themselves

One of the easiest and fastest ways to spot a narcissist is by watching how they talk. Narcissists love talking about themselves. As we have mentioned before, their image is everything, and because they are insecure, they tend to seek validation from other people. You will find them talking about themselves, their accomplishments, or their looks. They believe that they are better and smarter than you, and you will be able to sense it in their tone. However, not everything a narcissist tells you is the truth. They want to be admired, so they will exaggerate some, if not all, the stories they tell. Even if they haven't accomplished much or have no success stories to tell, they will try to impress you with their future plans. They also like to show off, which is why they have expensive tastes and will brag about their celebrity friends or the expensive restaurant they go to. All of this is an act to mask their insecurities and emptiness.

A narcissist loves hearing themselves talk, and they have no interest in what you have to say. If you find yourself speaking to someone who constantly talks about themselves, loses interest when you start talking, interrupts you, or makes anything you say about them, then they are probably narcissists.

On the other hand, some narcissists can be very attractive and charming with many interesting stories to tell. They will let you talk and pretend to be interested in what you have to say, but this is a manipulation technique to lure you in. Eventually, they will lose interest in you, and it will become all about them.

They Don't Have Empathy

If someone doesn't have empathy and cannot feel other people's pain, they may be narcissists. Imagine you are telling someone a sad story, and you can tell from their face that they feel nothing, or worse, give you a rude or insensitive comment. You will probably think that something isn't right with them. Having a conversation with a narcissist will make you feel uneasy because they cannot understand human emotions. This is why most narcissists don't have successful relationships, which takes us to the next point.

They Don't Have Many Friends

As you know by now, narcissists use and manipulate people to get what they want and to feel good about themselves. This is why many of them don't have real friends, as they cannot forge a real connection. You will notice that all the people in their lives are just colleagues and don't have any long-term or real friendships.

Sense of Entitlement

According to the narcissist, there is nothing more important than them. They are the sun, and the whole world revolves around them, and you should treat them as such. They expect you to cater to their needs; you will only eat the food they love and watch the shows they enjoy. Being in a relationship with someone like that will feel one-sided since they only care about their needs and what they can get from you.

Using Other People

Narcissists see people as means that help them get what they want. This may not be something you will spot early on, though. However, the more you know the narcissist, the more you will start feeling used and exploited. If you are in a relationship, you may feel that they are only using you for sex, or if you work together, you may notice that they are taking credit for your work. You will also see them bragging about how they managed to take advantage of someone like it is something they are proud of. Narcissists are hunters, and you are their prey.

Always Right

You will never be able to debate with a narcissist or even have a fair fight with them, and if you try, it can be emotionally draining. This is because a narcissist is never wrong, so sometimes arguing with them will feel like talking to a wall. You won't get anywhere with them because a narcissist doesn't listen to you, understand you, admit when they are wrong, and they will never compromise. They are right, you are wrong, and that is it.

Arrogance

Narcissists are arrogant, and they believe that they are better than everyone. However, deep down, they know that they are worthless. They will be rude to security guards, waiters and look down on anyone less fortunate than them. For instance, if they get the wrong order at a restaurant, they may be rude and even hostile towards the waiter. This can be a huge red flag, showing how they will treat you in the future.

Envy

Narcissists are extremely envious. They will never be happy for anyone or celebrate someone's success. They always want to be the best, and if they feel like someone is better than them, they will tear them down and say that this person doesn't deserve their success, even if this person is a partner, child, or parent. Additionally, if you try to criticize them, they will accuse you of being envious because, in their minds, they are so great and perfect, and everyone is jealous of them.

Narcissists are bad people, and if you get close to them, they can destroy you and ruin your life. They are miserable and filled with self-loathing. They crave drama, pain, and suffering, and putting people down is how they feel good about themselves. You may think that this is an exaggeration and people can't be that bad. However, this is your good nature talking. There are many terrible people around us, many of whom are narcissists. Do you know that most serial killers are narcissists? They lack feelings and humanity and don't think the rules apply to them. So, when you spot a narcissist, do yourself a favor, run as fast as you can, and never look back.

Chapter 4: Effects of Gaslighting

Gaslighting is not only physically exhausting but can also be psychologically and emotionally draining for the victim. Being subjected to this toxic, manipulative behavior can have short and long-term effects on the victim. Whether it's scapegoating or reality manipulation, every kind of gaslighting can pose a threat to the victim's health and comes with repercussions. While learning about the signs of gaslighting is important, you should also know the effects and consequences of exposure to gaslighting and how to deal with a gaslighter.

This chapter will discuss the emotional, psychological, and physical consequences of experiencing this abusive episode for years.

Depleted Self-Confidence and Self-Esteem

Gaslighting can majorly affect a person's self-esteem and self-confidence. The abuser targets the victim's weaknesses and vulnerabilities, which makes them question their own existence. They feel that they are not good enough and believe every accusation projected by the abuser. They may also feel powerless, alone, and intimidated. As they continually hear the accusations, blames, and negative comments, the victim starts believing that they are not good enough. Words like "crazy," "strange," and "insane" may also be constantly thrown, which can seriously damage the victim's self-esteem.

When the victim is being manipulated, they fail to recognize the toxic traits of the gaslighter and instead blame themselves for being too sensitive. They convince themselves that the problem lies in their incompetence and they are too simple-minded to comprehend the situation. A similar train of thought often leads to depleted self-confidence. Over time, the victim may also fear expressing their perceptions and emotions. They feel that they are passive, weak, and unable to accomplish any task. They believe that they are not the same, that their assertive and strong selves have vanished into thin air.

Since the abuser can go to great lengths to keep their toxic trait hidden, the victim often fails to recognize the signs early on, which leads to disbelief and self-loathing. The manipulator often adds in a dash of charm to cover their reality, which overshadows their derogatory remarks and attitude. They have a way to twist their words and blame every mistake on the victim instead. The manipulator fails to respect the victim's decisions, emotions, and opinions, which decreases their confidence.

Drained Social Life

When a person suffers from low self-esteem and self-confidence, they automatically isolate themselves and keep away from others due to the fear of being judged and manipulated. In some cases, people who are already socially disenfranchised fall into the trap of manipulators and gaslighters, further affecting their social lives. Typically, victims do not like meeting new people as they believe that they will be manipulated. Whether it's a private party or a corporate event, they despise almost every kind of social gathering.

Maintaining a social life is important for personal and professional reasons. Everyone needs a strong network to rely on. Social interactions can enhance your mental health to a great extent. It fosters your psychological and emotional health as well. Being Social and part of a group is a necessary human trait that can help strengthen personal bonds and define your identity. You may say that you are "introverted" or do not like to socialize a lot. But, let's face it, even introverts feel the need to communicate and share stories with their loved ones. At one point, every human needs to interact with others to maintain their physical, emotional, mental, and psychological health.

Due to excessive manipulation and constant bickering, people around the victim may also perceive them as incompetent, unaware, and fragile. If the victim notices minor behavioral changes in people around them, they may feel more overwhelmed and start overthinking. With an already declined self-confidence, they may also not be able to confront the gaslighter or their loved ones who misinterpret them. They also fear being misjudged due to a lack of communication skills. In the end, they give up and avoid confrontation altogether, which is why they avoid social gatherings.

Poor Decision-Making Ability

Victims of constant gaslighting also tend to doubt themselves over and over again. Since the gaslighter projects the disbelief of incompetence and ineptitude, the victim starts believing that they are actually not proficient enough to make decisions and take control of their own lives. Typically, gaslighters target people who seem vulnerable and possess low self-confidence. Some gaslighters even suffer from narcissism or borderline personality disorders, which increases their radius of victim hunting and leads them towards defenseless groups of people. They feel superior by manipulating others and demeaning the victim by making them feel dull, timid, and feebleminded.

This, in turn, increases self-doubt, and the person ends up believing that they are too frivolous to make decisions. From choosing the meals to eat to making important investment decisions, the victim may face trouble making any kind of decision. In a way, gaslighters portray that they are too important for the person, and any decision made by the victim cannot be validated without the abuser's presence. This leads to increased dependency as well, even during the most important stages of the person's life. Since the gaslighter questions each and everything said and done by the victim, they may also show that they are superior and can make better decisions.

If you are being gaslighted, second-guessing yourself is a common trait. With low self-confidence, you are unsure and insecure about your skills and abilities. Some gaslighters are specifically keen on propelling their choices and making them a priority. In a relationship, the gaslighter may always prioritize their needs and wants by belittling their partner's choices. Choosing a holiday destination, picking a restaurant to eat, or buying furniture, the gaslighter will always decide by making the victim aware of their "poor choices" or "bad taste."

Having a stance in a relationship is important to some degree as it helps balance the partner's thoughts and decisions. However, if it crosses the threshold, it can be labeled as gaslighting, directly impacting the victim's decision-making ability.

Increased Vulnerability

Even though the victims feel that they are being manipulated and the gaslighter is juggling their emotions, they still keep trusting them, which can lead to increased vulnerability. Despite knowing the facts, they feel helpless and cannot do anything about it. In most cases, the person's dependency on the gaslighter is simply baseless. However, they are either scared to face it or prefer to live in denial. The inability to trust themselves also stems from this behavior.

Other than the abuser, the victim fails to acknowledge the efforts and help given by their loved ones and well-wishers. This is also the case with the ones scapegoated by abusers. They know that they are fed false information by the gaslighter but are unable to take action. In fact, they question their own thoughts and decisions. This is majorly seen in relationships and marriages. The gaslighting partner often makes the victim feel that they are walking on eggshells, making them more insecure.

If you find yourself in a similar situation, beware of the gaslighter's requests as they can easily manipulate you into doing their tasks. Whether it's housework requested by your gaslighting partner or taking on an extra project requested by your manipulating colleague, you need to be wary of these instances and draw boundaries. Do not let others take advantage of your vulnerability, which is why you need to recognize the gaslighting signs as soon as possible.

The Inability to Trust Others

This toxic loop of increased vulnerability and the inability to trust others can be exasperating for the person. With constant gaslighting exposure, the victim isolates themselves even more. They believe that every person they meet will do the same and manipulate them. However, for this effect to occur, they first need to realize that they are being or have been gaslighted. If not, they are simply vulnerable and seamlessly allow others into their life. Coercive control is one of the most dangerous signs of gaslighting because it is difficult to decipher this pernicious behavior.

Signs of coercive control include checking your partner's phone and activities to keep a close eye on their daily life. The gaslighter will always keep an eye on the partner's movements. If they spot any unusual activity or behavior, they will instantly question them. They may even threaten them to speak the truth (even if there is no truth to be revealed and the partner is innocent). This is what gaslighting is- even if the victim is innocent, the gaslighter will force them to spill out facts and prove that they are, in fact, wrong. When the victim realizes that they are being monitored at every step and gaslighted thereafter, they lose trust in everyone else as well. Needless to say, no one wants their privacy to be invaded, especially by the people close to them.

If your partner is gaslighting you, it is, of course, difficult to acknowledge this negative experience and come to terms with it. You may constantly question your decision about choosing this kind of partner- the one who you thought was loving, kind, and perfect. In turn, you will not only question your perception but also doubt others. Are they really who they show they are? In the long term, not trusting others can also put a dent in your precious relationships. However, you may feel that you have a solid reason not to trust someone, which can weaken the bond you share.

People-Pleasing Behavior

You assume that people do not like you simply because the abuser has labeled you as "insensitive," "weird," or "not good enough." You may be trying to maintain a relationship with your loved ones, but the newly developed negative self-perception may hold you back. If the gaslighter is jealous of the victim and talks negatively about them in front of others just to demean them, the victim may get triggered and fight to retain their image. Those who rarely care about what others think are at peace because they know who they really are. This also stems from the constant practice of self-love and calmness.

On the flipside, victims with low self-confidence and self-esteem are barely at peace. They think that no one likes them, and their loved ones believe the claims projected by the gaslighter. This triggers people-pleasing behavior, and they go all in to prove that the gaslighter is wrong. However, since the gaslighter has a way with words and actions, the victim will likely be unsuccessful. They will still continue to please people with their actions and words. If someone is important to them, they may also become possessive and try their best to retain their good image. Over time, the victim and their loved ones may, in fact, separate or stop talking.

As you can see, some victims stop socializing, and others try to get closer to their loved ones. This difference boils down to whether or not the victim has deciphered the toxic traits of the gaslighter. Once they know that they are being gaslighted, they may try to get closer to their loved ones for protection because they fear losing them.

Physical Health Issues

People often forget the physical health issues that can develop due to the effects of gaslighting because they are more focused on treating the mental issues. In a way, mental and emotional abuse can take a toll on their physical health as well. It can plague your health in every form and at different levels.

Some unfortunate victims also fall into the trap of physical abuse. If the gaslighter is aggressive, they may often take it out on the victim by beating or physically abusing them. If the victim is too scared to speak up, they may hide the truth from others and put up with the physical abuse. Needless to say, it can majorly affect their physical health and cause internal injuries as well. In some cases, victims are also forced into sexual activity, leading to physical injuries.

The constant mental pressure and emotional abuse eventually show on the victim's body. They may look leaner, tired, and pale. You can instantly tell that something is bothering them or that they are unhappy.

Distorted Reality

The victim may have a distorted view or illusion about reality after years of gaslighting abuse. Since the manipulator constantly lies to them, they cannot tell if the abuser is finally speaking the truth. This is a common form of emotional abuse in gaslighting. They may also forget their true sense of self or who they are in reality. The manipulator's influence clouds their needs, wants, expectations, anticipations, opinions, thoughts, and emotions. Sadly, this emotional abuse keeps growing and triggers other negative emotions over time. The victim may even feel pangs of sadness, anxiety, and even loneliness, especially in public.

Most gaslighters lie to cover their bad and manipulative behavior. In fact, lying becomes a part of the gaslighter and victim's life. The gaslighter keeps throwing in lies to cover up their previous deceit, and the victim gets more confused when searching for the truth. They become so immersed in this loop that they fail to recognize the reality. At one point, they are unable to distinguish between their real and imaginary life. This is known as the "Twilight Zone," wherein the victim believes that every dimension and situation is surreal. If they feel that a certain situation is not real, they may also act out, believing that no one will judge them on the other plane.

Disbelief, Denial, and Defense

Disbelief and denial are the first stages of falling prey to gaslighting. The victim wonders if the gaslighter is causing trouble or whether they are the real problem. Surprisingly, the victim may not even ask the gaslighter but doubt themselves, thereby going into denial mode. They trust the abuser, which results in disbelief, shock, and pain. If they catch the manipulator lying, you may still struggle to prove them wrong. For example, if a person sees their partner with someone else and is convinced that they are cheating on them, they may not reach the truth. In a way, the gaslighter may end up blaming their partner for not trusting them enough or being the weakling in the relationship, which leads them to cheat.

Some victims still try to resolve the situation to exit their toxic relationships, which is when they gather evidence and ask their partner many questions. This is when the victim reaches the second stage of their gaslighting trauma- the defense stage. Their partner may not cooperate and refuse to answer the questions too. However, the victim may still try to unravel the truth and force themselves out of this abusive relationship.

From here, the victim may probably be able to reveal the truth or get sucked deeper into the gaslighting whirlpool. In the former case, the person can find a concrete reason to get out of the relationship and end it. However, this abusive period can lead to depression and feeling overwhelmed and exhausted (especially if they have been exposed to gaslighting for several years). In the latter case, they are caught in the same situation they have been in until now.

Increased Mental Health Concerns

Over time, gaslighting can impact the victim's mental health and lead to several disorders like isolation, depression, anxiety, or any form of psychological trauma. With low self-confidence, increased vulnerability, and a drained social life, the person may feel more anxious and agitated. If left untreated, the situation can worsen, leading the person towards dark depressive episodes or even anxiety attacks. Typically, mental health concerns build up when the gaslighter's insidious behavior is not recognized or acknowledged.

If left untreated, the person may also be subjected to drug abuse and alcohol addiction. Depression, which, if also left untreated, can lead to suicidal thoughts and self-harming. Some victims feel hypervigilant, which means that they may develop an exaggerated fear of every situation. They fear that they are exposed to danger and are therefore careful in every situation. This fear multiplies if their partner is physically abusive when they are angry. They may be at the receiving end of physical abuse and forced sexual activity at any point in time. This aggravates their fear, especially if they feel trapped in the relationship and believe there is no end. Posttraumatic stress disorder (PTSD) or any other form of psychological trauma is also a common effect of long-term exposure to intense gaslighting.

As mentioned previously, gaslighting is not just common in relationships and families but also society. Every kind of gaslighting and manipulative behavior can have different kinds of effects on the victim. For example, immigrants often face racial gaslighting in foreign lands, which makes them more anxious. Trivializing racial comments, criticizing their identity for feeling superior, and denying important events and cultural implications are some subtle signs of racial gaslighting. If the indirect racial abuse continues, they may also get trapped into depression, eventually leading them to leave the country.

Low self-confidence, isolation, poor-decision making skills, and the inability to trust others add up to create a serious mental health issue, which can be dangerous for the person in the long run. As you can see, all these negative effects and repercussions of gaslighting are interlinked. They can take a toll on the victim's physical health, professional life, and even financial status in the long term. It is necessary to recognize the signs and effects of gaslighting early on and treat them as soon as possible. Failing to do so can cause irreversible damage for the victim in every sense. Some people fail to realize that they are being gaslighted, which is why it is necessary to decipher the physical, emotional, and mental effects of this toxic behavior.

Chapter 5: Recognizing Gaslighting before Recovery

We have talked in earlier chapters about emotional abuse and how it can be subtle, making it hard for the victim to recognize the abuse. Since gaslighting is a form of emotional abuse, it can take the victim a long time to realize what is going on. Imagine if, every time you fight with someone or confront them about something, they contradict you, shift blame, or deny what happened. At first, you may think that the gaslighter is probably right. Maybe you don't remember exactly what happened, or maybe this whole thing was really your fault. Why would a loved one lie to you? Eventually, when you keep having your memory and perception of things contradicted, you will start questioning your sanity and second-guessing yourself. This is what the abuser wants, to weaken you so they can easily control you.

Most people think gaslighting is associated with romantic relationships. However, gaslighting can take place in different areas of your life. A family member, friend, or co-worker can be gaslighters. Politicians can be gaslighters as well. The term was used a lot during Donald Trump's presidency. A narcissistic man thinks he is always right and happily denies facts when it serves him. Cult leaders are also known to employ this technique to get people to follow them, like serial killer Charles Manson who was known for leading a cult and murdering people. This is how dangerous and even deadly gaslighting can be.

Gaslighters are smart, which is why they take their time to employ their technique. It is done gradually so the victim doesn't suspect they are being lied to and controlled. Some people don't understand why the victim doesn't leave when they start questioning their sanity or they feel that something is wrong. This is because the victim doesn't understand that they are being abused. Even when questioning their sanity, they still have no idea that this is a form of abuse.

The impact of gaslighting can be damaging to your mental health. You are basically living with someone who makes you feel that you are losing your mind. You need to get away from this mental and emotional torture and seek help to be able to live a normal life. However, for you to heal and start the journey towards your recovery, you will first need to recognize and understand that what you are going through is gaslighting.

How to Recognize Gaslighting

Constant Confusion

As we have mentioned before, gaslighters want to confuse their victims and make them question themselves and their perception of reality. Therefore, if you feel that you are always confused and that you are losing your mind, you are a victim of gaslighting. Deep down, you probably feel that something is wrong with your relationship and the person you are with. This is your gut feeling telling you something, so listen to it. Being in a relationship should make you happy, not miserable and confused all the time. This isn't right, and you know it. You should be in control of who you are. If you find yourself slipping away, then clearly, you are in a toxic situation. Healthy relationships don't feel like this.

Gaslighters also use another technique to confuse you by being nice, caring, or loving every once in a while. This is a form of manipulation to try to convince you that they aren't so bad. Again, a healthy relationship should be good and positive all of the time, even when you fight. If you can count the times that they have been nice to you, or you use these moments to convince yourself that they still have good qualities, then you are being gaslighted. Relationships are easier and simpler than that, and they don't include any confusion or mind games.

Questioning Your Reality

Are you constantly questioning yourself and your reality? Do you keep asking yourself if a certain event or situation actually happened? If the answer to these questions is yes, then you are a victim of gaslighting. Being in a toxic and abusive relationship for a long period can take a toll on your memory and perception of reality. In time, you will find it hard to remember certain events or how something exactly happened. This is a result of the constant lying and denials you have been subjected to over the years.

Feeling That It Is All Your Fault

If your partner is constantly lying to you and hurting you while making you feel that you are the one causing them pain, then this is definitely gaslighting. They may hit you, insult you, call you names, and control you but somehow make it seem that you are the aggressor. They will say things like, look what you have made me do, or this is all your fault. There is no excuse for abuse, and you know this. The way they are treating you reflects who they are, and it is most certainly not your fault. If they have succeeded in confusing you and making you believe that everything is your fault, you need to self-reflect. Just compare your life to theirs. Who has lost more people? Who has had to compromise more? Whose needs aren't being met? If you are the one whose life has completely been altered while theirs is still the same, then they are definitely the aggressor.

Isolation

When was the last time you had lunch with your best friend? Do you remember the last time you called your siblings? If you haven't been in touch with but your partner in a long time, you are being isolated from your loved ones. It may have happened gradually with the excuse that these people want to ruin your relationship or any other insane reason to keep you apart from your loved ones. A healthy relationship doesn't require you to give up the people in your life, but a relationship with a gaslighter will.

Fear

Are you constantly afraid of your partner or parents? Do you avoid talking about your feelings out of fear of being accused of overreacting? Do they blame you every time you fight? Are you afraid of their frequent angry outbursts, so you watch everything that you say and do? Do you constantly put their feelings first while they dismiss yours? If you answer yes to all of these questions, then you are living with a gaslighter. In any healthy relationship, couples fight without feeling they are at war, and someone has to surrender. You shouldn't be silenced out of fear. It is perfectly normal to talk about your feelings and discuss any issues you may have.

"This Isn't Me"

You will wake up and look in the mirror one day, and you won't recognize yourself anymore. Although nothing physically has changed about you, you will still feel that this isn't you. Every word you say, every action you take, and everything that you feel will make you say, "This isn't me." When you feel that your identity is withering away, this is a huge red flag that something isn't right. This is your gut feeling trying to tell you that your relationship isn't healthy. Even feminists who are strong and independent can fall prey to this type of relationship. However, this isn't your fault, and you aren't weak. You are simply a victim of a manipulative unstable person who is gaslighting you. A healthy relationship should never make you feel this way.

Recognizing that you are being gaslighted may not be so easy since you are under someone else's control. However, if you feel that something is off, then you are probably right. Even if you can clearly see all the signs, it may be difficult to believe that you are being gaslighted. It can be very painful to realize that someone you love and trust can do this to you and that you have been lied to and deceived for years. Even when you leave the gaslighter, you will still feel hurt and heartbroken, and that's okay. Grieving a bad relationship, even a toxic one, isn't wrong. It is actually a part of your healing process.

It Is Okay to Grieve

It may feel weird to grieve a toxic relationship. People will tell you that you should be happy and celebrate your newly found freedom. You may face judgment from some people who can't understand why you are missing your abuser. However, you shouldn't feel bad for feeling this way. Getting out of a toxic relationship will require a lot of healing, and the first step in your recovery process is grieving and coming to terms with what happened. You still lost someone you cared about and ended a relationship or a friendship, even if it was bad. Endings are always sad. Unlike grieving a healthy relationship, grieving a bad one can be complicated, exhausting, and conflicting but still necessary. You need to understand why you are grieving or, more precisely, what you are grieving.

You Miss the Good Times

As we have mentioned earlier, from time to time, a gaslighter will treat you nicely. It is a part of their manipulation tactic, ensuring you won't leave them. Looking back fondly at these memories and missing them is very normal. You have loved this person even though they were toxic and, at times, dangerous. You simply miss someone you used to love and share loving memories with, however small they were. That being said, don't expect your loved ones to be very understanding. They have seen you being hurt, abused, and isolated from them, so your grief won't make sense. They may even be angry that you are mourning this person's loss. In this case, you may need to speak to a therapist or another toxic relationship survivor to make you feel that your feelings are validated.

You Suffered So Much

You aren't only grieving the end of your relationship, but you are also sad for yourself and what you have endured. You have suffered so much, and no one knows this better than you. You had to repress your feelings, hide your anger, and question your reality. All of these things have negatively impacted your mental health. You have basically given up your voice and identity to please them. You wore the clothes they chose for you, styled your hair the way they liked, and weren't allowed to have an opinion. In addition, you took the blame for all their mistakes, were isolated from your loved ones, and your confidence was shattered. These are all things that you are grieving. You are sad for yourself and for everything that you had to endure. You need this, you need the grief so you can move on.

It is okay to grieve. You need to grieve the person that you loved or at least who you thought they were. It is normal to feel sad. You have endured a horrible experience that, more often than not, makes you question your sanity. Take your time and grieve but ensure you do that in a healthy way, like going to a therapist or finding a support group of toxic relationships survivors that can help you move on. You aren't grieving them, you are grieving for yourself and this is the first step towards healing.

How to Grieve a Toxic Relationship and Heal

Understand Your Feelings

Right now, it may be hard for you to understand your feelings. You have been repressing them for so long that it may feel like you are getting reacquainted with them. Additionally, being a toxic relationship survivor, you may have strange emotions that you don't really understand, especially since your feelings have been masked for so long. In other words, you could never express how you were feeling accurately, so you are used to expressing something while you mean another. You may find yourself having angry outbursts every once in a while. However, what you are really feeling may not be anger. You may be feeling hurt that you loved someone who was incapable of love, or maybe you are ashamed of yourself for being in a toxic relationship in the first place. Part of your grieving process is to understand your feelings and get to the root of the problem. You can write down everything you feel and try to understand the reason behind these feelings. For instance, if you get mad at someone, ask yourself if you are really mad at them or yourself.

You will also experience different feelings at the same time, maybe even on the same day. For instance, you may wake up feeling grateful for getting out of this toxic situation, but you may feel sad and miss the person later that day. This is normal and a part of the grieving process.

Be Sad

Cry, write in your diary, or listen to Adele, do whatever you need to do when you feel sad. Give yourself time and space to simply be sad and grieve. You need to feel these things because repressing your sadness can delay your healing. Be sad, so you can heal and move on.

Go No Contact

Narcissists are known for trying to get back with their exes, not because they love you but to satisfy their ego and see if they still have power over you. They will try to manipulate you to get back with them or tell you they want to stay friends. As you know by now, narcissists don't have friends; they only use people. They want you in their life because they aren't done using you yet. You are in a vulnerable state, so going no contact will help speed up your healing. Block them on social media and change your number if you must. Remember that this is someone who has manipulated you for so long, so they know your weaknesses and what buttons to push. Even if this person is a parent or a sibling, you still need to distance yourself from them and avoid them completely.

You may want to stay in touch with them because you want closure. While this is normal, you should know that you will never get closure from your abuser. Narcissists and gaslighters will never admit any wrongdoing, let alone apologize for hurting you. They may have actually convinced themselves that you are the one that hurt them. You will get closure by finding your way back to yourself.

"Gaslighting"

At the time, you probably didn't understand exactly what you were going through or even had a word for it. Now that you know that you have been gaslighted, it is good for you to use the word "gaslighting" to talk about your experience. It will help you better understand what you have been through.

Surround Yourself with People You Love

Normally, you will want to spend time alone to be sad and evaluate your feelings. However, you need to also surround yourself with the people who love you, whether it's friends, family, or a loving partner who definitely wasn't the gaslighter in your life. . You need a support group to remind you of your old self and to get to trust in yourself again after spending a long time questioning your reality. You also need your support group in case you are tempted to call your abuser. They can be there for you to listen and talk you out of contacting them.

See a Therapist

You haven't been through something easy. You reached a point in your life when you were questioning your sanity. This is why you will benefit a lot from seeing a therapist. They will advise you on how to grieve and guide you towards your recovery properly. Therapy will also help you get back to your old self and learn to trust yourself while building your confidence. A therapist will also help you learn to express your feelings in a healthy way after masking them for so long.

Accept That the Relationship Is Over

Acceptance has always been an important part of moving on. You need to accept the fact the relationship has ended. Unlike healthy relationships, toxic relationships can make you feel like you are high on drugs, making you tempted to go back to the gaslighter. This is why you need to acknowledge that it has ended and accept it so you will never be tempted to go back.

Take Care of Yourself

After spending a long time catering to someone's needs, it is time for you to take care of yourself and your needs. Do all the things you used to do before the relationship that made you happy. Eat your favorite food, binge-watch your favorite TV shows, listen to music, or travel. Getting back to your old self and interests will help you feel normal again.

Forgive Yourself

It can be easy to blame yourself for what happened to you. You may feel anger and shame for not leaving sooner or for allowing someone to use you like that. First of all, you should know that being gaslighted wasn't your fault. You need to know that and believe it. You can't keep blaming yourself. Gaslighters are experts at manipulating people, and you had no way of knowing. You should be grateful that you managed to recognize the abuse and get out when you did. So instead of being harsh on yourself, try being kind and using positive words. Treat yourself the same way you treat your best friend or sibling when they have made a mistake. Be kind, compassionate, and forgive yourself. You aren't the first person to be manipulated by a gaslighter, it can happen to anyone.

You should also avoid using words like a victim, as it may not be helpful to see yourself this way. You are a survivor who managed to get out of an impossible situation and are on your way to recovering.

Take Your Time

You need to be patient with yourself and accept that the road to recovery may be long. People heal and move on in different paces, so accept that and don't compare your journey to anyone else's. You will also need to accept that there will be days when you are going to be just fine while other days you will feel it all over again. This is normal, and healing is complicated and will take time, but you will eventually get there.

It may not seem like it now, but you will get back to your old self. Or maybe you will emerge out of this a new person, a better version of yourself. You will be able to feel like your normal self and learn to trust again. Recovery takes time and what you have been through isn't easy. Before we move to the next chapter, you should take a moment and pat yourself on the back and be proud of yourself. You are a survivor starting the healing process, and you are on your way to recovery.

Chapter 6: Gain Confidence and Move Forward

At its core, gaslighting is manipulating a person's reality and perception, and, out of everything, that is what damages us the most. A gaslighter starts their work with their victim by love-bombing. They bombard their victims with love, recognition, and appreciation while pushing for intimacy (emotional/intellectual) very early on in the relationship. Of course, when written like that, this type of relationship feels disingenuous and forced. However, gaslighters are really good at making this first phase feel like the greatest love story ever told. This earns the victim's trust, and that is when phase two starts.

After a gaslighter has placed themselves as a source of validation (which comes easily if the gaslighter is a parent, teacher, or superior), they start making their way towards becoming the only source of validation. Meaning they slowly chip away at your own sense of approval, judgment, self-esteem, self-confidence, and most importantly, your perception of yourself.

Over time, their constant and persistent effort results in damaging one's relationship with themselves. As a result, you may start doubting yourself, your instincts, memories, and abilities. You may also stop looking to yourself for guidance, even when it comes to the simplest decisions in life. As you stop listening to and validating your own wants, needs, and experiences, this self-abandonment will create a lot of tension between a person and themself.

Randy is a little boy who lives with his gaslighting mother. Every time he asks for a new toy, his mother replies with, "You don't ever get enough, do you? You're so ungrateful." Eventually, he's bound to learn that asking for a toy is futile because his caretaker won't provide it. It won't take him long before he discovers that the only way to get his mother's attention is through aggressive behavior.

Now, while you are not a gaslighter, being in contact with one can cause you to internalize their voice, gaslighting yourself to an extent. Needless to say, when you start gaslighting yourself, your mind labels you as an enemy, the same way Randy's mind reacted to his mother. Instead of trusting you and speaking your needs - "I feel scared, I need safety." - your mind is more likely to be critical and harsh - "You're so weak. You're a spineless pushover with no personality."

Healing is about restoring our trust in ourselves. It's about repairing the internal damage done by the gaslighter and rebuilding something stronger instead. This chapter will explore how to heal by restoring our trust, confidence, and sense of self. That way, you can rebuild a healthy internal environment where you can feel safe, loved, and supported.

Your Current Internal Environment

Healing the relationship you have with yourself starts with recognizing the current state of affairs on an external level, as we discussed in the previous chapter, and on an internal level, as we will be discussing now.

This list of questions will guide you towards a deeper understanding of your internal environment:

- **Do you consider yourself and yourself to be on the same team?**

Being on the same team not only means having the same goal, but it also means walking down the same road towards achieving this goal.

Maggie suffers from a generalized anxiety disorder, although she has been getting better at managing her emotions for a while. On a particularly bad day, her anxiety took over, and she ended up snapping at her partner, which deeply hurt them. She apologized and her partner completely understood. However, on her way home, she felt a deep sense of shame and self-hatred. A critical voice rang in her head, "You're a failure. They deserve so much better than you."

Anxiety is an uncontrollable stress response to danger or perceived danger. If a bear is attacking you, what would be your main focus, surviving or being respectful? Having a generalized anxiety disorder can sometimes mean being stuck in this survival mode (physically, emotionally, and mentally) for no apparent reason. Now, picture functioning normally while trying to override your brain's survival mode - while trying to convince your mind that there are no metaphorical bears in the city. It's exhausting. You're bound to get tired. The feelings are also bound to get overwhelming at some point because, just like gaslighting, anxiety disorders alter your perception of reality.

Ultimately, Maggie's main goal is to live life fully without allowing anxiety to negatively impact her life. Being on the same team means offering compassion and understanding to the self and vice versa, instead of turning to violence, shame, blame, and self-hatred to achieve this goal.

- **Imagine yourself as a human being independent of you. How would you describe your current relationship dynamic?**

It's common among gaslighting victims to have a turbulent relationship with themselves, although the differences lie in how the abuse impacts the individual.

Some may describe their relationship with themselves as being around someone they feel is incompetent and shameful. This could indicate underlying feelings of guilt/shame because you couldn't recognize when you were being abused or couldn't defend yourself, even though it really is not your fault.

Others may feel like their relationship with themselves is abusive, with the self being malevolent to an extent. This could signify a wounded self who feels unsafe communicating their needs or asking for attention. It could indicate the existence of a big rift in the shared trust between you and yourself.

Meanwhile, others may feel like their self is a burden to them like they can actually live their lives if only themself and their fears, emotions, and needs didn't stand in the way. If you can't see these as your own fears, emotions, and needs, this could indicate a severe disconnection between you and yourself.

Keep in mind that there are endless types of relationships and relationship dynamics, so don't restrict yourself to the three examples we mentioned. As you explore the relationship between yourself and yourself, keep your mind open, stay curious, and try to refrain from judging. This is simply an exercise in observation.

- **To what extent do you trust your thoughts, emotions, instincts, and overall experience of an event?**

This question is a good way to assess the damage done to your confidence and self-trust by a gaslighter.

The effects, and therefore answers, will vary, depending on the type of relationship, the severity of abuse, and the amount of time spent around the abuser.

To get the most accurate answer, refrain from going to either of the two extremes: having no trust or being fully trusting. Revisit several situations and observe them to understand the level of trust between you and yourself. This means looking for whether or not you trust yourself and the factors that affect this trust.

Repairing the Rift

What Caused the Rift?

The wounded part of you is similar to a child. It needs to feel safe, seen, heard, accepted, and loved by the rest of you. It also needs to be nurtured and cared for. Being involved with a gaslighter means that you don't have the ability, capacity, or the willingness to meet those needs.

If your physical and emotional safety is entirely dependent on the unpredictable whims of a gaslighter, to stay as safe as you can, you'll try your best to please them. Because a gaslighter is only pleased when everything goes their way, your independent existence is bound to upset them. As you learn the keys to keeping a gaslighter 'sedated', you gradually start losing touch with yourself and what you want and need.

As you lose touch with yourself, a part of you begins to lose its trust in yourself. This can show up in the form of social anxiety due to not trusting yourself to protect yourself if need be. It can also show up in angry outbursts due to thinking that you wouldn't be able to communicate normally.

It is important to state that the rift in trust is not your fault, and neither is staying in a relationship more than you should have. You did your best with the level of awareness and the capacity you had at the time, and right now, you are trying to heal yourself, which shows that you truly care.

The rift in trust is a result of having suffered persistent and powerful manipulation that is extremely hard to spot unless you already know what to look for. In the big picture, however, whose fault it is doesn't really matter.

What matters is this:

You have been through trauma that forced you to disconnect from many parts of yourself for all of you to survive. Now that you're taking steps to push the gaslighter out of your life, it's time for you to repair the damage done.

To heal, it is up to you to rebuild a safe environment for yourself and start acknowledging your hopes, dreams, desires, needs, and emotions. It is also up to you to rebuild the trust that has been shattered.

How to Repair It

Regardless of how turbulent your relationship with yourself is, there is always hope for repair. Now, the journey may be long, and it can sometimes be challenging, but it is not impossible. More importantly, as you heal, you'll notice yourself getting lighter, feeling better, and existing more freely than ever before. The key is to take it step by step, hour by hour, and day by day.

The repairing process is all about consistently showing up for yourself. That way, gradually, you'll be re-earning your trust in yourself.

Freddie has been in and out of relationships his whole life. Woman after woman has betrayed him in more ways than one. After he swore off relationships, he found himself falling for Jasmine. Jasmine truly loved him, and she showed it without ever giving him a reason to worry. Nevertheless, Freddie would often find himself distrusting Jasmine's feelings and her as a partner.

Freddie, however, knew that his feelings were a result of his many negative experiences and not because of Jasmine. Instead of starting fights or running away from the relationship, he decided to observe Jasmine. He saw the time she made in her week for him, the many ways in which she showed him he was wanted, accepted, and loved, and how much effort she put into keeping their relationship healthy. Gradually, his view on relationships started to change. He began to feel comfortable trusting in her love instead of having a blind conviction that the love is bound to go away.

This is reparation in action. Although, for yourself, it's a little different than with a partner.

For yourself, rebuilding the trust starts with:

- Adopting a kinder, healthier manner of inner dialogue: The way you talk to yourself is everything, especially after being in a hostile and critical environment for so long. The way you talk to yourself shapes the way you see yourself, combats your inner critic and allows you to trust in your consistent self-love.

- Setting aside some 'me' time: Quality time is time set aside for yourself, to rest, to have fun, to play, to get to know yourself, to reconnect with the child within you, to reconnect with nature, etc. How you spend your 'me' time is up to you: read, write, draw, take a walk, go to the beach, listen to music, dance, sculpt, or binge-watch your favorite show. The key is consistency, so don't commit to what you can't handle - you can start with as little as five-to-ten minutes daily and work your way up to a system that fits your life. This will help you create a safe space for yourself that you can depend on and trust. More importantly, it will help the wounded part of you see that it is valued and loved.

- Making space for your emotions: After having been through such a tough time with your abuser, it's normal for you to have a lot of feelings regarding this experience. As you start connecting with yourself, these emotions will come out naturally when you make space for them. This part may be difficult, but allowing yourself to feel the emotions is the only way to let them go and fully heal. Be present for yourself, express those emotions in your way, and practice self-care. This will help you create a sense of emotional safety for yourself.

Self-Perception, Confidence, and Self-Esteem

Self-esteem, confidence, and self-perception are three interdependent psychological resources that get severely impacted as a result of gaslighting. As we've previously mentioned, gaslighting discredits one's self-perception, robbing them of their ability to see who they are with their own lens. It also robs them of their confidence and ability to trust what they see. Self-esteem is one's confidence in their own value, which gets reduced to nothing because of consistent abuse and degradation.

If you're reading this book, it means you already have some trust in your perspective on reality. It means you've noticed that something is wrong and have decided to take action and make changes. It also means you've decided that your time and energy are valuable enough for you to defend them against trespassers. This is all to say that self-perception, confidence, and self-esteem are all resources that you possess and have always possessed. Your gaslighter may have affected how you connect with these parts of you, but they did not and cannot impact these parts directly. That's why the next part is not about regaining but reconnecting.

Shedding and Reconnecting

Reconnecting with your self-perception is simple, but shedding your abuser's perception of you is the challenging part. The good news is, the process requires you to do both shed and reconnect, which means that the process will get easier as you start practicing it.

While you were with a gaslighter, you may have seen yourself from their perspective. Regardless of how good or bad, their point of view wasn't grounded in reality. It was sculpted to serve their own motives and goals. So, why should you choose to see yourself using someone else's invalid and severely limited point of view instead of your own? More importantly, why should you give it more power and credit than your own point of view?

As you go about your day, notice how you see yourself, as well as the voice of your inner critic. Do you identify with this point of view? Does the voice speaking in your head sound like you, or does it perhaps sound like someone else, particularly your abuser?

As you examine your existing self-perception, you'll find that some of the things you think about yourself are things that have been said and confirmed to you by your abuser. Keep in mind that some of these things can also stem from your own insecurities and your own experiences. That's why the first step is close examination. That's how you know what to shed and what to keep.

The second step is to reconnect with your own self-perception. In other words, how do you see yourself? This step is all about asking yourself questions and observing yourself in interactions.

- Who are you (not what you're good at or your assets or your likes/dislikes)?
- What are qualities that you like about yourself?
- What makes you feel happy/sad/scared/angry?
- How do you show love?
- How do you accept love?
- What are you good at?
- What are you not good at?
- What parts of you would you like to work on?

The answers you receive from these questions and your observations will help you reconnect with how you see yourself. When old perceptions come up - when you hear the voice of your inner critic - all you need to do is challenge them. They are not facts. You have the facts, you have the deepest understanding of yourself, and only you can see yourself fully.

Confidence: A Natural Outcome

As you start to see yourself from your own point of view, you'll automatically start noticing the gaslighter's flawed perspective. It'll suddenly dawn on you in the form of, "Wait a minute, that's not true."

Remember, confidence doesn't mean they are right. Gaslighters have an abundance of confidence but none of the facts. You have the facts, and as you realize that your facts are evidence-based and as real as the sun and the moon, you'll notice your confidence growing.

What you can do is support yourself and empower your views. Don't put yourself down. Don't doubt yourself either. Keep an open mind for new information and deeper self-knowledge.

Self-Esteem: Trust Is Key

Two action sequences go into building/reconnecting with your self-esteem, both of which take effect when supported by your confidence in your self-perception.

The first sequence involves recognizing your value, challenging your negative beliefs about yourself, and exploring your identity and qualities.

The second sequence involves acting based on your updated and healthier self-perception. If you've noticed that you are smart, allow yourself to speak in situations where an opinion or a point of view is required. If you believe that you can handle a specific professional challenge, put yourself out there and pursue it. If you believe in the value of your time and energy, put up boundaries with those who drain you and uphold them.

Acting on your beliefs will further cement them and empower you to trust in yourself.

Now is the time for you to heal, move forward, and start rebuilding, but you cannot build a city without building gates to protect it from trespassers. The next chapter is dedicated to helping you build solid boundaries that will hold against any gaslighter and will also help you protect yourself, your time, and your energy.

Chapter 7: Boundaries and Healing

Gaslighting is a complicated form of emotional abuse, as we have already discussed at length in the previous chapters. Abusive relationships involve chronic manipulation that will leave the victim feeling exhausted. Basically, it undermines the sufferer's perception of reality and creates destructive self-doubt. The abuser or gaslighter will constantly try to spin their harmful, negative, and destructive narrative and behavior in their favor and will often will deflect the blame onto the victim. So, even though the victim is the one suffering abuse, the gaslighter would make it appear as if they behave that way because of the victim. Consequently, the person suffering this type of abuse ends up feeling mentally unstable, paranoid, unhinged, or silly and may not have the confidence to carry even the most mundane tasks or take the simplest of decisions. Gaslighting is the most tragic of all abuses because it slowly eats away at a person's confidence, and all they are left with is an empty shell of themselves.

Taking Action Is Imperative

Gaslighting works like a toxic web and paralyzes the victim through constant emotional abuse. The abuser is literally controlling the victim and making them feel paralyzed. Not only that, but the abuser also actually convinces the victim that they deserve the abuse because of their own wrongdoings. All of this is extremely debilitating and damaging for the mental well-being of the sufferer.

Taking swift and timely action is important for the victim's well-being. One of the most important steps to take towards healing is setting boundaries. However, they are also quite tricky and hard to implement because the abuser would resist with all their might. Therefore, setting boundaries is quite crucial if you wantto resist taking on this abuse. Since boundaries are essential to the healthy functioning of your relationship and your own sanity as an individual, it is important to set them clearly and effectively without any delays. Boundaries often make people feel a bit uncomfortable, and for this very reason, many of us usually avoid setting them. Even if we have thought of boundaries, we usually procrastinate when it comes to implementing them. This is most often the case in intimate or romantic relationships, and it is a very tragic reality.

Regardless of the type of relationship you have with a person, boundaries are paramount, and they matter a lot and apply to everyone in our life. Boundaries are a must in a relationship ridden with gaslighting and other types of abuse, but they can be very difficult to implement. This is because boundaries serve the function of fences or protective borders that safeguard our psychological well-being and emotional strength. Boundaries are also a way to communicate to others the behaviors that we expect of them and protect us from the possibility of abuse and manipulation around us.

There are "no and never" zones for everyone because no one can do everything asked of them. Otherwise, the world would have devolved to chaos ages ago. Everyone has limits and different expectations from everyone because there are things that you may feel are appropriate, and there are things you may not be willing or ready to accept. As with many things, it is not at all easy to establish boundaries and maintain them in a gaslighting relationship because the abuser will make it difficult for the victim to follow through.

Why Are Boundaries Important?

Boundaries serve the purpose of a rule or guideline for others to interact with you to make you feel safe.

For the victim of gaslighting, it is extremely important to be brutally assertive and honest about the boundaries they want to incorporate and to clearly and regularly communicate those boundaries. If the abuser or the gaslighter is showing insolent disrespect for those boundaries, you must be firm about enforcing them. One way to do that would be to limit access to the victim or avoid the abuser. However, before we start discussing more establishing boundaries in a relationship, it is important to understand why boundaries are so important.

As we have already discussed, healthy boundaries are needed for well-functioning relationships and are important for self-care. Without any boundaries, you may feel walked over, depleted, or taken for granted. It is not only required in intimate relationships but in any relationship you have. Understandably, for different relationships, you will have different types of boundaries. More importantly, boundaries need to be laid out clearly because poorly established ones may end up leading to resentment, anger, or burnout.

Another important function of boundaries is to enable us to create a protective and self-care space for ourselves by allowing us to refuse things that we do not want to do or indulge in. It is all about creating a clear line around what we feel okay with. We can broadly categorize boundaries into two types:

1. Healthy Boundaries

These boundaries would help protect a person's self-respect and self-esteem while also protecting emotional and physical space against unwanted intrusion. They also create a healthy relationship by creating opportunities for mutually shared power and responsibility. With clearly set boundaries, the person can feel confident about agreeing or disagreeing with something. It would also empower a person to make healthier choices and to be responsible for themselves.

2. Unhealthy Boundaries

One classic example of unhealthy boundaries is not clearly stating what you want or not being clear enough about the limits. This would also mean that the person has a weak sense of identity and lets others make various decisions in their life. That person may also feel powerless and would shed off any responsibility. As you may gauge from this unhealthy behavior, these boundaries are good for nothing and cannot benefit the individual or their relationships. It will often create more chaos in the relationships and make them feel helpless and resentful.

It is quite common for people (even if they are not abusers) to resist boundaries, and you would find it's never an easy job to establish healthy boundaries. You have to understand that when you start implementing them, there will be attempts where people around you will test those boundaries to see how far they can make you resist. You must keep in mind that setting boundaries is not wrong, so you need to assert the boundaries you have set for yourself in a relationship.

As Gerard Manley Hopkins says, *"Your personal boundaries protect the inner core of your identity and your right to choices."*

Why Would Someone Violate a Boundary?

It happens more commonly than we would like to accept, however, abusers or anyone who violates another person's boundaries may also be suffering from insecurities and identity issues. This means that they get in the habit of boundary violations because they feel inferior to the other person (in this case, the victim) or needy. The abuser may also feel that the victim is, in reality, a lot stronger and would often forget or ignore that a victim is a living person who has human vulnerabilities and needs. Sometimes, both the victim and abuser have failed to establish personal boundaries, resulting in a toxic and unhealthy fusion of personal spaces that is not good for anyone involved. Not only is such a relationship unhealthy, but it is also very non-functional and unproductive.

Another possibility could be that the abuser may actually be suffering from a psychological disorder or ailment that limits their understanding of the other person's personal space. One of the examples is someone who has a personality disorder, like narcissistic or borderline personality disorder, that demonstrates a general disregard for the boundaries set by another person because of excessive self-focus and self-absorption. Another reason is when someone has neurological impairment in areas required for social cues or social perception.

Various Areas to Establish Boundaries In

There are various areas where boundaries must be established or are applicable. In general, four important areas require clear and exclusive boundaries:

- Mental or psychological

- Physical

- Emotional

- Spiritual

In addition to understanding the applicable areas, you also need to understand that boundary violations can be of internal or external types. The boundary violations of external nature usually deal with physical space, for instance, it could be about an unwanted touch or standing too close. A good example of this would be someone taking something out of your purse or bag or personal space without asking your permission first. This is an outright violation of your personal space and demonstrates an infringement of external boundaries.

On the other hand, the internal boundary violations have to do with feeling responsible for another person's (most likely the abuser or gaslighter, in this case) behavior, thoughts, or feelings. The internal violations involve assumptions around being aware of how the other person would feel, or think and this is quite insane to expect of anyone at all times. These violations also revolve around how a person should act around the abuser. As a rule of thumb, it is helpful to keep in mind that whenever someone is covertly manipulating or coercing you to do things or dictating how you live your life, they violate your boundaries. Another infringement of internal boundaries that often go unnoticed or may not seem like a violation is when the abuser makes the victim feel responsible by blaming them for how they (the abuser) are feeling.

However, in reality, having personal boundaries is a basic human right, and everyone is allowed to have them. Setting boundaries need not be an invitation for a guilt trip from anyone, whether they are intimate or romantic partners, parents, siblings, friends, or coworkers. Moreover, as individuals, everyone should feel comfortable and assertive about the boundaries they have chalked out for themselves in the relationships, and a violation or threat to those boundaries could be a sufficient cause for leaving that relationship.

Boundaries in Gaslighting Relationships

Establishing boundaries is hard, even in normal relationships. This is particularly difficult because gaslighters are usually people in your life who you value, love, and are attached to. These individuals (abuser or the gaslighter) are also people you are involved with in close relationships (these relationships may or may not be intimate). Below are some of the ways through which you can establish healthy boundaries even in gaslighting relationships.

1. Create Some Distance

It is important that the victim establishes boundaries before it is too late, and to do that, it is important to detach oneself from the gaslighter. It is not easy to create distance between the victim and the abuser because the abuser is not a stranger. Unfortunately, the gaslighter or the abuser is a close loved one, and it becomes hard to avoid interactions with that person or to cut them off completely from the victim's life.

Distance will help the victim get a new perspective and be free of the pressure that has accumulated because of staying in the abusive relationship. This space may not seem much, especially if it is just a figurative one, but it is quite powerful. Because as soon as the victim breaks out of the pressure and noise, they will discover peace and moments of quietness and calm that they can enjoy and savor.

This distance or space would also be intuitive for gathering their thoughts and reflecting on important milestones in life. The victim also gets a chance to process their thoughts and emotions on a daily basis through this. In short, this distance is so much more than just a space between the victim and the gaslighter because it is the "breathing space" in an overly suffocating and toxic relationship dynamic.

2. Communicating Effectively Is the Key

Communicating your boundaries doesn't have to be about being harsh or rude because it is not about starting an argument with the abuser or gaslighter. Moreover, rude communication strategies often end in resentment because they invite reactivity and defensiveness from the other person. Instead, it is better to communicate the boundaries with compassion, love, and politeness, but this does not mean you have to give up being assertive. Taking a soft start is the key here because the goal should be to avoid as much criticism and contempt as possible (however, it is understandable that this may not always be the case in an abusive relationship). It could be as simple as saying, "thank you for asking me about this. I would appreciate it if you continued asking me before using this".

3. Add Some Trick Words

Now, this may not work all the time in an abusive relationship, but it sure does help soften up the tone and purpose of the statement a little. The trick is to replace the word "but" with "and also". This helps create a tenderness in the speech, and the listener gets the message that both things can coexist. So, saying something like, "I always enjoy our time together, and also that it's unsettling when you are late. So do inform me if you are going to be late." The statement conveys the message but with a tinge of softness.

4. Psychobabble May Be Switched

It is possible to simply state that you need boundaries in your relationship, and there is nothing wrong with saying that. Remember, the goal here is to avoid getting entangled in a direct conflict with the gaslighter because it will only invite more toxicity for the victim. You may say that "I feel quite uncomfortable with (XYZ), and I need (XYZ)."

5. Take Ownership

Often, when people set boundaries and communicate them to others, they make it sound like blame. In an abusive relationship, when you stand up to a gaslighter to protect yourself, this may be the case, but it is important to avoid the toxicity associated with it. Moreover, taking ownership is taking away the factor of blame and giving you the responsibility of establishing those boundaries, and it is quite empowering to feel capable and powerful enough. So, without hesitation, take ownership of your boundaries and proudly state that you are setting those because you need them instead of saying that the abuser is making you do so.

6. Shed Light on the Positive Aspect of Boundaries

It is important to make the other person see how boundaries can be positive and healthy for both parties. Since they are also vital for the health and longevity of a relationship, it may be quite intuitive to talk about that as well. This discussion sheds a positive light on boundaries and frames boundary setting in a productive and healthy perspective.

7. Stand Your Ground

The tricky thing about gaslighters is that they make every attempt to get you to feel guilty. It is quite common for an abuser to make the victim feel that they should already know the feelings of the gaslighter and how the boundaries or a certain reaction (from the victim) made the gaslighter feel. In this situation, the victim should firmly and assertively stand their ground because it is not their responsibility to know how the gaslighter (or how anyone feels for that matter). Saying "no" to a request or an invitation by a person (the abuser or gaslighter in this situation) does not deserve a bad reaction or tantrum.

Setting boundaries is always a struggle and a process, even in a healthy relationship. When it comes to a relationship suffering from the most toxic forms of emotional abuse, everything becomes more challenging. However, this does not mean that the victim or sufferer should give up trying. Not standing up to the abuser is the worst thing that the victim can do to empower them. It is also important to remember that you do not want to engage in an argument or lash out at the abuser because it is ineffective and may escalate the conflict.

It is intuitive to remember that you need to accept, change, or leave a situation, and it simply means that you are accepting the patterns and changing your boundaries or leaving the abuser. No matter what your course of action may be, the important thing is to always see and recognize the violations. The journey of establishing effective boundaries in an abusive relationship is difficult, but it's possible.

Chapter 8: Self-Compassion and Self-Care

When it comes to your healing process, you need to prioritize healing and self-love over everything else. We realize that introducing self-compassion into your life after years of hating yourself can seem impossible. However, it is possible as long as you keep showing up for yourself. Self-care is an essential step in recovering from an abusive relationship where you were gaslit for so long. Your abuser probably tarnished your self-esteem and sense of self. This is why it is really important for you to deliberately indulge in the acts of self-care until it seems like second nature to you. It may seem difficult to even think about being compassionate towards yourself, but it will only get easier. This chapter discusses what self-care means and the strategies you can use to incorporate the acts of self-care into your routine.

What Does Self-Care Mean?

Self-care refers to the acts of self-love, where you indulge in conscious efforts to make your physical, emotional, and mental health better. It is important to understand that self-love does not entail the same meaning as being self-absorbed or selfish. Self-care only refers to taking care of yourself in a healthy way that will allow you to complete your chores and do the work needed. Acts of self-care help us live a healthy life without relying on anyone else to fulfill our emotional needs. When it comes to the victims of abuse, it is extremely important to consciously indulge in the act of self-care and compassion to get in touch with yourself. Self-care gets things done and aids the treatment of your depression and anxiety. Self-care can refer to a task as simple as putting lotion on your dry hands as it shows how you are listening to your body and taking care of its needs. Taking care of your nutrition, social needs, bodily needs, medicinal needs, sexual needs, or even need for space are all considered acts of self-care.

How Can Self-Care Aid You in Your Recovery from a Gaslighting Relationship?

It is common to lose your sense of self after being stuck in a toxic relationship where you have constantly been gaslit and manipulated for years. It causes your self-esteem to deteriorate, leaving you feeling hollow and crushed. When recovering from an abusive relationship, you must try your best to indulge in acts of self-love and develop compassion for yourself. Remember, it is completely fine not to have your life together all at once. You may struggle to get on your feet right. However, it is completely okay to take as much time as you need. Taking baby steps still counts as progress. Prioritizing yourself will help you regain control over yourself. Making conscious efforts to be kind to yourself while taking care of your needs will help you rebuild your strength. Taking care of yourself is also great for the recovery of your self-worth. Having self-compassion can accelerate your process of healing from a toxic, gaslighting relationship.

Strategies for Self-Care

Learning to be comfortable with the acts of self-love and self-compassion can take you some time. Making conscious efforts to be kind to yourself after years of abuse and manipulation can be tough. Especially when your gaslighter makes you believe that you are not worthy of love and appreciation. In this section of the book, we will discuss some strategies for self-care that will help you ease into your new healthier lifestyle. Starting with little acts of love and appreciation towards yourself can prove quite fruitful in the long run. You need to start small and then take it forward gradually.

Exercise

Incorporating physical exercises into your routine can do wonders for your mental and physical well-being. It will not only help you get back in shape, but it also relieves you of stress and anxiety. Physical activities are a great way of releasing tension from your body. Being in a relationship with a gaslighter can cause you to fall into depression. Depression goes after your will to live and causes you to stay in and indulge in binge-eating, sleep for longer hours, or just binge-watching movies while snacking on unhealthy foods. Exercising will help you lose the extra pounds you may have gained from stress-eating or lack of activity due to depression. It is also possible that you may be going through an opposite situation. Depression and anxiety work in different ways. No two people are the same. You may have lost weight due to the loss of appetite and extreme stress. Exercising is great in this regard as well as it helps you gain muscle mass and build strength. Make sure to go easy on yourself and start slow.

Self-Care Requires Time and Effort

Even the idea of taking care of yourself after months or years of hating yourself can seem impossible. Like everything else, it will take you time to get used to being loving and kind to yourself. Self-care requires a lot of time and effort. Toxic relationships can cause you to lose your will to dress up and look good for yourself. It may seem like a lot of effort at the start. That is because every little effort will feel laborious, especially when you're so used to not taking care of yourself. However, it is important not to give up. Stay consistent in your efforts, and one day you will reach a time when taking care of yourself will feel like second nature to you.

Give Yourself a Break

It is important to not give up on yourself and take as much time as you need to get used to taking care of yourself. There will be days when you will think that it's impossible to get better and be happy again. But, be a little more patient, and you will reach the pinnacle of self-compassion and self-love that you should aspire to achieve.

Acknowledge and Reaffirm Your Value

After being broken and gaslighted for such a long time by your abuser, it is important to remind yourself how wonderful you are. You must reaffirm your value by saying kinder things to yourself and remembering all the great things about you. You are a complete and whole person with amazing qualities that overshine your so-called flaws. Your gaslighter may have only focused on your flaws. They may have made you believe that you will never be good enough for them. But it is not true. Gaslighters are usually manipulative narcissists who have deeply-rooted insecurities. They will always project their insecurities on you, making you believe that you will never be good enough.

Tell Yourself How Wonderful You Are

After years of listening to your abuser hurling hurtful things at you, you may have started believing those things yourself. Gaslighters, treat you like a jewel at the beginning of the relationship, but it gradually changes as the relationship progresses. This is why it can be shocking for you to make sense of the change in their attitude towards you. It may cause you to believe the awful things they say to you. However, you must know that there is nothing wrong with you, this is just their way of gaining power over you. They will never accept the blame and will always make you believe that you're inferior to gain control over you and ensure that you never leave them. This is why, now that you are free or trying to be free from your abuser, you must regain your lost sense of self. Your gaslighter's definition of you doesn't define you.

Just Breathe

Breathing exercises have proven to help a lot with stress and anxiety. Whenever you start to feel depressed and anxious, remember to take a moment to practice breathing exercises. It will help get your heartbeat to slow down. Whenever you feel overwhelmed or feel that you're on the verge of a panic attack, remember to do some breathing exercises to regain control over your emotions. Breathing exercises are as simple as sitting down, closing your eyes for a few seconds, and breathing in through your nose till the count of four. Then hold your breath till the count of 7 and then exhale through your mouth to the count of 8. This is called the 4-7-8 breathing technique. It is proven to calm your nerves when you feel overwhelmed or out of control.

Healthy Eating

Eating healthy is an act of self-care. Eating healthy food means that you honor your body enough not to fill it with junk food. Even though sugary, fried, and salty foods are considered comfort foods, they are not good for your body if consumed every day. Moreover, unhealthy food can lead to feeling lethargic and lazy. Sugar is quite addictive. This can hinder you from cutting out sugar altogether if you consume large portions of it. This is why you must introduce healthy food such as green vegetables, salads, good carbs, and protein into your diet to take care of your physical health. Not only that but healthy eating is also linked to improved mental health. It will help you feel stronger and more energized than ever before.

Share Your Story

Sharing your story with the people you trust will empower you. Once you're finally ready to share your story, the feeling of being held by your past will not keep you captive anymore. You will be free from the shackles of your past. By sharing your story with others, you will feel more in control of the narrative. You will be sharing your side of the story with others. This way, you will not be allowing your gaslighter's twisted version of the story to overshadow the truth.

Be Honest with Yourself

More than anything else, you must be honest with yourself. Being honest with yourself means that you will allow yourself to feel the emotions you're going through, no matter how difficult they may be or how bad they make you feel. Feeling your emotions and not lying to yourself will help you move on and make peace with everything that has happened. You can journal your feelings and write a poem or a song- whatever helps you understand your honest feelings about yourself. Being true to who you are and not lying to yourself is the ultimate act of self-love. It will allow you to be compassionate and loving towards yourself.

Journaling

Journaling is an excellent way to deal with your grief. It is also a great act of self-care. Writing down your thoughts in a journal or a notebook will help you make sense of your feelings and thoughts. You must be feeling hurt even after getting away from your abuser. Sometimes it gets difficult to make sense of our own emotions, and you may not be able to talk about it with your friends. Journaling gives you an outlet to express your feelings and emotions without any worry. You can pour your heart out in your diary or journal without thinking twice about it. When you freely let the words take over you, you get your thoughts detangled and understand some things that may have seemed foggy or confusing to you before. Writing serves as a wonderful way to acknowledge your difficult emotions and create a safe space for you. It relieves stress and anxiety and keeps you from getting depressed. Journaling is an amazing act of self-love and self-compassion. You not only allow yourself to feel things but also give yourself room to understand yourself and relieve yourself from the complex emotions that have been weighing down on you for so long.

Volunteering

When you give to others, you attain a feeling of satisfaction and peace. Volunteering is a way for you to help others in need. While volunteering, you feel like you have a purpose in the world, and many people could use your help. It makes you feel worthy and useful- something that your gaslighter may have led you to believe that you're not. When you volunteer for the less fortunate in society, you feel blessed and feel grateful for everything you have. You also feel the need to help them with all you have. You can also volunteer at rehabilitation centers for abused women. This can help you share your story with others and listen to theirs. You will gain strength and feel liberated. Volunteering is a great way for you to spend your time as it allows you to work with humble, kind, and compassionate people in society, and you get to learn so many different stories. You will feel truly at peace.

Take a Break from Social Media

Taking a break from social media is a great way to break away from the anxiety and stress that society puts on you. Social media can be a great way to connect with other people and stay updated on the latest news. However, sometimes, it can be too much for you to handle. Too much information, especially negative information, can drain you. If you are already going through a rough patch, even a little bit of negative information can be a trigger. This is why sometimes, taking a break from social media can be healthy. Disconnecting from the world for a little while can prove to be fruitful. While trying to heal from your wounds, you can deactivate your social media and focus on your healing. You can take this time to do some journaling, take up new hobbies and learn new things. We tend to spend so much time on our phones. You can use that precious time towards healing yourself and getting better. When you feel you have the energy to deal with people, you may activate your account and catch up with your friends and family.

Continue Therapy

Therapy is an act of compassion and love for yourself. Therapy helps you make sense of your situation, and your therapists provide you with healthy coping mechanisms to deal with stress and anxiety. When you choose to continue therapy, you choose to show up for yourself every day. Therapy keeps you from relapsing and falling back into your toxic patterns. It also helps you deal with the complexities and aftermath of your separation from your gaslighter. You will be experiencing things on your own after a long time of being held emotionally captive by your gaslighter. It is possible that you now question your worth and ability to do anything after your gaslighter undermined you and made you believe that you will never be good enough. This is where your therapist comes in. Your therapist will teach you strategies to work on regaining your self-esteem and will equip you with tools to help you achieve your goals. It is important to continue therapy until you become stable and regain control over your self-esteem, emotions, and life in general. Remember, you are the real hero in your life, and your therapist is only there to guide you and help you get better.

Set Goals

Setting goals is a healthy way for you to make progress towards your future. It gives you a sense of purpose and gives you a feeling of accomplishment. You can try and set SMART goals for yourself - SMART stands for small, measurable, achievable, relevant, and time-bound goals. You can set goals that vary from day to day, or you can set weekly goals. Setting goals keeps you from staying in bed and wallowing in self-pity. By setting goals, you will be able to get your work done with enthusiasm. You can give yourself rewards for achieving your goals on time. For example, you may treat yourself with dessert or a present when you successfully complete a task. This will help you stay motivated and stay on track with everything that needs to be done. Setting goals for yourself and successfully achieving them instills a strange feeling of happiness in you that is addictive. After some time, setting and achieving goals will become easier for you. This is the ultimate act of self-care as it helps you feel better about yourself.

Having self-compassion and self-love for yourself, especially when you feel like you're in the darkest of pits, is a major act of bravery. You need to be kind to yourself and remember that this journey of learning to love yourself again may take you some time to get used to. However, as long as you keep showing up for yourself, you're good. You must remember that you deserve to be treated with love, respect, and kindness. No one is going to love you and care for you as much as you. You're the one who stood up for yourself and took yourself out of the toxic relationship. You had to go through that every day. You did not give up on yourself, even when you wanted to the most. You are fiercely fighting your negative thoughts and emotions every second of the day. You are a fighter, and you need to reaffirm your value every day to remind yourself how amazing and courageous you are. Learning self-compassion and self-love will help you get through difficult moments in your life. Remember to be there for yourself, and you will be just fine.

Chapter 9: Future Relationships

Part of healing requires one to develop healthier relationships. After the rough period that you went through, it is natural to want a fresh start. Forming new relationships with people who were not a part of your painful past can do wonders for your healing process. It allows you to move on and gives you a chance to be happy and explore the new part of yourself. Building healthier relationships will be easier, considering that you now have a healthier perception of yourself. You can create healthier friendships when you view yourself from a place of self-love and compassion. However, it can still be difficult to form new relationships and trust people again after being gaslit and abused. This chapter discusses ways to form new relationships with your friends, romantic partners, and family members while maintaining healthy boundaries.

Advice on Establishing Healthy Relationships after Narcissistic Abuse

Opening Up Slowly

To heal from abuse and establish healthy relationships with others, it is important to open up slowly and share your story. It will clear the fog regarding your abuse and will clear everything that happened with you. Moreover, it is also important for you to tell your own story to free yourself from the baggage you're carrying to your new relationships. It will also help them as friends and potential partners to recognize and avoid your triggers.

Do Not Get into a New Relationship Right Away

When you get out of an abusive relationship, it is natural to feel vulnerable. You may want to seek relief and comfort in someone else. However, it is crucial to strictly avoid getting into a new relationship. There are higher chances of you attracting another narcissist as they like to prey upon the people who may be recovering from a toxic past. This is why you have more chances of getting stuck in the same pattern as before. Taking a break from getting into a new relationship will help you focus on your needs completely and know yourself better. Once you know yourself better, you will have a better chance of starting a healthy relationship with someone more compatible.

There Are Good People in the World

It may seem at the moment that everyone around you is a villain because the person you trusted the most, gave your all to, turned out to be nothing like you thought they were. At this time, you must surround yourself with people who genuinely care for you, like your friends and family. They will remind you that there are still good people in the world that you can trust and turn to when you need to be comforted.

Establish Boundaries

If someone exhibits toxic behavior, you must establish strict boundaries right then and there. You must tell them that this sort of behavior will not be tolerated. It may be hard to be this stern and first, but you must get used to setting boundaries. If someone violates them after repeatedly being warned about it, it is clear that they do not care about your feelings. Toxic people benefit from your lack of boundaries as it helps them take advantage of you. Establishing boundaries will filter the manipulative people out of your life.

Punish Toxic Behavior

It is important to take a stand for yourself and punish toxic behavior after clearly defining your boundaries. Abusive and manipulative people benefit from separating you from the people close to you. Hence, whenever you feel like a friend or partner is trying to separate you from your loved one, you must discourage this toxic behavior. You should not let anyone sabotage your healthy relationships and stay away from them till they apologize or fix their behavior. If they repeat it, you must tell them to stop, or you will stop engaging with them.

Avoid Your Triggers

You must try your best to disengage with people and activities that trigger your bad memories. It is absolutely fine for you to look out for yourself, even if it means avoiding someone who triggers your painful memories. Your healing should be your priority, and you must take all measures to recover and be healthy again. You can even try telling the person about this, and if they care about you, they will definitely understand and honor your wishes. When you think you will be able to meet them again without triggering your hurtful past, you may continue to build your relationship with them slowly.

Talk to a Therapist

Your therapist will help you heal from your abusive past and help you build new and healthy relationships. Talking to your therapist will help you to focus on forming new bonds with people that are healthy for you. They may also help you recognize any toxic patterns or traits you may repeat in your relationship. They will also help you quit obsessing over your toxic ex or the abusive person in your life. It is easy to become fixated on them. However, you must concentrate on creating new friendships and exploring new relationships.

Form Healthy Friendships While Recovering from Gaslighting

Creating new friendships after a significant period of isolation may seem difficult at first. However, it is healthy for you to form new bonds with people unrelated to your past. Here is a list of things you should keep in mind when making new friendships after being gaslit and abused.

Take a Trusted Friend along When Meeting Someone New

Once you start developing new friendships, it is important to stay vigilant. You may want to take a trusted friend or family member when meeting someone new. They can help you identify if the person is genuinely nice or is just pretending. They will be viewing this new friend from a neutral point of view. This is why they will be able to help you in this regard. You will also feel more secure in the presence of someone you know. It will help you put your guard down and interact with the other person freely. This will help you form healthy new bonds.

Establish Boundaries

You must never allow anyone to cross boundaries, no matter how good of a friend they are. You can still be close to people without letting them violate your boundaries. Remember, you set your boundaries for a reason. You must honor them and ask others to do so if they want to remain in your life. Healthy friends will respect your space and boundaries. If they have your best interest at heart, they will even appreciate you for creating boundaries in the first place.

Give People the Benefit of the Doubt

It is normal to be paranoid and question everyone's motives when starting a new relationship. If someone is being nice to you, you may fall back into the old thinking patterns that drive you to believe that they must not be who they seem to be. However, you must give everyone you meet the benefit of the doubt and remember that not everyone you meet will manipulate you. There are good people in the world. It is healthy for you to be vigilant and form healthy boundaries. But you must not allow yourself to become paranoid and question everything someone does for you, as this will hinder you from creating healthy friendships.

Surround Yourself with People that Appreciate You

You must not underestimate the power of appreciation, love, and support. The people who allow you to be yourself and love you for it are the kind of people that you would want to have in your life. Surrounding yourself with people who appreciate you for who you are will help you gain confidence and will aid you in your journey of developing self-compassion and self-love. Building healthy friendships where respect and love are mutual will do wonders for your mental health and healing.

Form Friendships that Are Mindful of Your Past

It is important to form healthy bonds with people who respect your past. These people will be mindful of what they say. Such friends will avoid bringing up things that trigger hurtful memories for you. People that truly appreciate you and have your best interest at heart will not want to hurt you deliberately.

New Romantic Relationships after Abuse

It is important not to get into a romantic relationship right after getting out of the abusive relationship. However, once you have recovered enough from the past relationship and feel like you may be ready to find your potential romantic partner, you must keep a few things in mind.

Communication in a Healthy Relationship

Communication is key. This statement must hold some truth to it considering how commonly it is used, right? When you are getting to know someone, you must try your best to communicate everything. It must be made clear at the start of your relationship that everything should be communicated. Healthy communication will help you understand your partner and vice versa. When it comes to communication, you must acknowledge that non-verbal cues also count as communication. Make sure that your facial expressions, tone of voice are sending the right message to your partner that aligns with what you are saying. Communication is a two-way street. You must allow some time to talk out your problems, misunderstandings, and, most importantly, your triggers. Telling your partner what hurt you will help them be careful next time and not repeat the same behavior.

Be Clear about What You Want

As stated earlier, you must be clear about what you want before getting into the relationship. Once you know what you are looking for in a partner, it will help you find someone who can fulfill those needs. It is also essential for you to communicate those needs to your potential partner at the beginning of the relationship. You must also consider their needs and see whether you will be able to fulfill them. Being clear about what you want at the start will help you establish an honest relationship with your partner where your needs will not be neglected.

Set Boundaries in Your Relationship

Like any other relationship, you must ensure that you set boundaries in your relationship. This includes how you want to be treated, what you are comfortable with, and other things you believe need to be addressed. Creating boundaries and being clear about them will help you maintain a healthy relationship with your partner. They will also be mindful of the boundaries and try to refrain from anything that upsets you or violates your boundaries. If your potential partner does not respect your boundaries, you must be firm and clarify that this behavior is unacceptable. If they continue to repeat that behavior, it may be time to move on.

Talk about Consent with Your Partner

When getting into a new relationship, you will probably want to have a sexual relationship with your partner. This is why talking about consent is extremely important. It will help you understand what your partner is comfortable with. For example, they may not be as comfortable with having sex or indulging in sexual activities as soon as you are. They may need more time. Consent means that all participants are willing to be engaged in the act and that they may change their minds at any time. It will help you be comfortable in your relationship and take it as slow as you need to.

Work on Feeling Good about Yourself

Working on self-esteem and having a healthy opinion of yourself will keep you from getting into toxic relationships. When you feel good about yourself, you don't allow the other person to disrespect or violate you. Having bad self-esteem may lead you to believe that you "deserve" it. However, it is not true. No one deserves to be abused, no matter what you believe. Having healthy self-esteem will keep you from tolerating abusive behavior. Stay clear from self-deprecating jokes as it is not only bad for you, but it may also give others the signal that it is okay to disrespect you and make jokes at your expense.

Take Things Slowly in Your Relationship

Entering a new relationship can be an exciting experience. You are learning about another person, and there is a possibility that they may be witty, charming, and interesting. It may make you want to speed things up in your relationship. However, it may not be the best thing for you. No matter how good you feel, you must always take things slow in your relationship. You must give yourself enough time to understand the other person better. You must take your time and identify what makes them happy, sad, angry, what they like, how they live, their opinions about politics, and things that matter to you, etc. This will help you see whether you are making the right choice by taking your relationship to the next step with this person. It is always good to take things slowly rather than being hasty.

Spend Time Apart from Your Partner

Everyone needs their space and time. It is good to spend some time apart from your partner to do activities on your own. It will allow you to retain your sense of self and keep you from getting overwhelmed. It also keeps you from being too dependent on your partner. Hanging out with people other than your partner will help you both maintain a healthy balance and keep you from getting tired of each other.

Align Your Values

Before you get into a serious relationship, you must talk to your potential partner about their beliefs and values. It is extremely hard to make a relationship work if your partner's values are different from yours. It also depends on how important your values are to you. If you cannot compromise on your values, you may want to reconsider getting into a relationship with the person in question.

Relationships with Family Members after Abuse

Family can help you heal from your abusive relationships- that is, if your abuser is not your family member. Healthy family members can lend you the support you need to recover from your hurtful past. Here are some ways you can interact with your family after getting out of a toxic relationship.

Steer Clear of People Who Like to Cause Drama

You will always come across people who live for drama. You must stay away from them. These people are extremely insecure and like to cause drama just for fun. You must not get into arguments with them and try your best to keep yourself out of any toxic situation that will take a toll on your mental and physical health.

Gaslit by a Parent

If you are being gaslit by your parents, you must make it clear to them that this behavior will not be accepted. You must disengage with them if they continue to gaslight you. You must not allow anyone to mess with your head and make you feel like your feelings and experiences are not valid. Sometimes our own parents can be abusive towards us, deliberately or otherwise. This is why you must tell them to quit their toxic behavior.

Reach Out for Support

In difficult times, your family can give you the support you need. After a long time of abuse and manipulation, it is natural for you to feel vulnerable and need support. Your family can offer you comfort and support to get through this difficult period in your life. Their love and compassion can help you heal and get back on your feet quickly.

Set Boundaries

Just because someone is your family does not give them the right to violate your boundaries. You set boundaries for your mental well-being. Establishing boundaries with family members will help you maintain a healthy relationship while making sure that no feelings are hurt. Creating boundaries is great for others around you, as it lets them interact with you while making sure they don't cross any lines. The people who care about you will respect your boundaries.

Identify People You Trust

As much as we'd like for it to be true, not everyone in your family is reliable. This is why you must identify people in your family that you can trust. These are the people that you can rely on, who can offer you support and compassion. Talking to them about your truth will help you get things off your chest. You will be able to talk to them freely without any fear of misunderstandings or drama.

We realize that it may get difficult to develop new relationships, especially after going through a rough period. It can be difficult to trust others, and you may find yourself questioning everyone's intentions. However, you must allow yourself to get out into the world again and form new friendships with like-minded people who appreciate and accept you as you are. There are still many great people in the world who will restore your faith in humanity. It is healthy to form new friendships and seek out romantic relationships when you feel ready. However, before that, you must work on feeling good about yourself to keep anyone from taking advantage of you. You are the only person who is going to stay with you forever. Never let anyone make you feel bad about yourself. It is the most important relationship. One that you must always protect before building relationships with others.

Chapter 10: Help and Counseling

There are many ways to seek help in emotional abuse recovery, from general counseling to group therapy to individual sessions with professionals. There are so many different types of counselors out there that it can be difficult to decide on the best one for you and your needs. This chapter will explain some of the different counseling methods that may be beneficial during an emotional abuse rehabilitation period.

What to Expect When Seeking Counseling?

When victims decide that it is time to seek counseling, they may find themselves at a loss when determining which professional counselor or therapist will be the best fit for their specific situation. In some cases, counselors can have different types of specializations, so speaking with them directly about what you are looking for can help narrow down your search.

When searching through various counselors in your area, you will want to look at their professional experience and the type of counseling they provide when working with victims who have been emotionally abused. If possible, it's always best to meet them personally before deciding. This way, you will be able to determine if this professional counselor is the right fit and whether or not they can provide the type of support you need throughout your recovery process.

There are many different types of counseling methods available to victims during this time. It can be helpful to seek therapy through individual sessions, group therapy, or even by attending support groups where you can meet and talk with other victims who have had similar experiences.

Individual Therapy Sessions

This type of counseling involves one-on-one sessions with a therapist. This is beneficial for those who need more personalized attention or feel like they can open up easier to someone outside of their support network (friends/family). The counselor will listen to your experience and offer advice on how to move forward healthily after gaslighting.

What to Expect in Individual Therapy Sessions

During your first session, the therapist will go over confidentiality and privacy concerns to make you feel more comfortable. This is also a good time for you to ask questions about their experience working with other people who have been through this type of abuse in the past.

Some therapists may require that all sessions be paid upfront and in full. They may also require that you purchase a book or workbook to go along with your sessions. If this is the case, make sure you ask any questions regarding why they require these materials before deciding.

It can sometimes be difficult for victims of emotional abuse to trust someone new right away. It may take several sessions before you feel comfortable enough to open up fully about what has been happening throughout your relationship with this person. This is normal and should not be something that causes concern for a therapist as long as they are following ethical practices.

Benefits of Individual Therapy Sessions

Some benefits of individual therapy sessions include the ability to talk with someone outside of your support network who can listen and offer advice on how you should move forward. Therapists are trained in handling situations like this one, so they will know what is appropriate or not when giving feedback/advice for coping methods.

How to Find a Therapist for Individual Sessions

You could look into finding one online or in the phone book, asking your primary care physician, looking through community resources (like churches), and even talking to friends/family members who might be able to recommend someone they have worked with before.

Group Therapy Sessions

This is another option for those who need more support during their emotional abuse recovery period. A group therapy session usually involves about six to ten people with similar experiences of narcissistic abuse sitting together with one therapist leading the group discussion. It can be helpful to share what you are going through in a group setting because it allows for constant feedback, support, and advice from others who may have gone through similar struggles.

What to Expect from Group Therapy Sessions

During these sessions, you will be able to express any thoughts or feelings you are having. This is a good opportunity for victims of emotional abuse to feel understood by others who have been in similar situations and share their own coping skills/strategies.

Some therapists may require that all group sessions be paid upfront and in full, like they do with individual counseling sessions. They may also require that you purchase a book or workbook to go along with your sessions. Some people might find it difficult to open up in front of other people they don't know very well. If this is the case for you, it might be beneficial to try individual sessions with a therapist before trying group sessions.

Counseling Centers

Many cities have community programs and counseling centers that offer low-cost services to those who need them. These places usually have a sliding scale fee policy that means that those who can't afford to pay may be charged less for their services.

Therapy Center Considerations

The center's location should also play an important role in your decision, as you will want it to be somewhere close to where you live or work. If your schedule is very busy, make sure they have evening hours or that you can go in at a time outside of normal working hours.

The environment should also be comfortable and welcoming, so you can feel safe discussing anything without fear of judgment from others. In addition, it's helpful if the center is clean, well-organized, and gives off a positive vibe.

Support Groups

Like group therapy sessions, support groups allow victims to meet other people who understand exactly how they feel during this time. The difference is that support groups usually take place outside of a counseling center, and the people attending will be going through their recovery period on their own. The purpose is to help you feel less isolated and more connected with others who understand your story.

Be sure to seek out any form of counseling or therapy that best suits your needs during this time. No matter what, you will need to get back on your feet, and it can be helpful to have someone by your side who understands what you are going through.

What to Expect from a Support Group Session

At these sessions, you will be able to interact with others and share your feelings outside of the very small or negative social circles that may exist in other areas. You can also feel free to talk about what's going on at home without fear of judgment from anyone close to you, including friends/family members and romantic partners.

In addition, it's a good idea to have an open mind and be ready to receive advice from other people who have been through similar situations. It might also surprise you how much your negative mindset changes after speaking with others for just one session or two. In the end, it can provide a fresh perspective on how to approach your situation.

When you feel emotionally safe, it may also be helpful to share what happened with the group and see if anyone else has been through a similar story. In addition, many of these sessions will have materials that can help in providing additional guidance for victims who are just beginning their recovery process after being emotionally abused.

In the end, keep in mind that you will be able to take what works for you from this experience and leave behind anything else that doesn't align with your needs or beliefs. In fact, it might feel a little uncomfortable at first when talking about such personal matters with strangers. However, after time passes by and you continue to attend sessions, you will likely feel a sense of relief and reduced stress levels.

How to Find a Support Group

Your local health insurance provider may be able to provide you with information about support groups in your area. They might also have literature that can help point you towards these resources if they do not offer assistance themselves.

In addition, other organizations like the National Domestic Violence Hotline often provide listings of local centers or programs for victims looking to attend sessions.

Be sure that you are open-minded and ready for anything during your first session or two at any support group. While some groups may provide pamphlets about different types of abuse (or even topics like nutrition), others might allow participants to share their stories.

It's important to attend any group session with an open mind and be ready for anything! In the end, you will eventually discover what works best for your needs during this time in recovery.

What Mistakes Should You Avoid While Seeking Help?

The biggest mistake anyone can make is to assume they are alone. It may be easy for you to feel isolated and not realize that there are plenty of others who have been through similar experiences in life.

In addition, it's important to stay away from any decisions that could worsen your situation. In some cases, you might feel pressured to take on additional responsibilities. This could include anything from assuming a new role within the household or even taking up more financial responsibilities once shared with an emotionally abusive partner.

In most cases, these decisions will only serve as a temporary solution, and they may actually make your life more complicated later on down the line. It's important to avoid making hasty decisions, as it will take time for you to recover and process what has happened throughout your relationship.

What to Do if You Cannot Afford Professional Help?

If you cannot seek out professional help due to financial reasons, there are still plenty of options available for victims. For example, once you have opened up about your past experiences with family members or friends in recovery, they might be able to provide advice that can help during this time.

In addition, it never hurts to attend any local support groups available in your area. These groups may also have information on various counseling services that you can take advantage of to help improve your emotional well-being during this period.

In the end, keep in mind that there are plenty of free resources out there for victims who cannot afford professional assistance or even group support sessions. All it takes is a little bit of research, and you will likely be surprised at the number of options available to you in your area.

There might also be certain experiences where they may not want to seek help from others, resulting in feelings of frustration or even loneliness over time if it goes untreated. These issues can often become worse when left untreated, which is why it's important to speak up about your feelings and experiences.

What Are Some Counseling Methods Provided?

One of the most common counseling methods provided during sessions with a counselor or therapist is cognitive-behavioral therapy (CBT). During these types of sessions, you will work with an expert who will help guide you through a series of techniques to help improve your overall mental health.

In addition, there are also other options such as Eye Movement Desensitization and Reprocessing (EMDR) or Narrative Exposure Therapy that may be provided during sessions with a professional who has been trained in these methods. These counseling approaches can help you work through past experiences and negative emotions that you may be feeling, which can help improve your overall mental health.

What to Expect during the Counseling Process?

The counseling process is different for everyone. In some cases, it might last a few short weeks, while others will need more time throughout their recovery period. It's important to recognize that the counseling process is all about you and what works best for your own unique situation.

In addition, it's important to give yourself time throughout the actual counseling sessions before coming up with expectations or setting deadlines on when certain milestones should be achieved. While some additional responsibilities may need to be handled right away, such as a new job search, if necessary, it's important to remember that the counseling process should be about you and your needs.

In many cases, victims may feel pressured by loved ones or even friends in recovery who have been through a similar situation when they were suffering from an emotionally abusive partner. In most cases, these counselors will do their best to avoid comparisons or judgments when working with you during your sessions.

Even if the counseling process lasts for a few weeks, it doesn't mean that all of your emotional issues will be resolved in this short period. It is normal to continue feeling emotions throughout the entire recovery process, as there are often residual effects after experiencing any type of abuse.

What Can Counseling Not Do for You?

Even though there are many benefits to seeking out a trained individual who can help provide counseling sessions, this doesn't mean that they can fix you. During therapy sessions, it is important to recognize the fact that they are not a magic solution. Your emotional scars won't heal overnight.

In addition, even though counselors have received extensive training to help provide counseling sessions, they cannot fix all of your problems during the recovery period. Sometimes it might take some additional time to work through these issues and emotions, which is why you shouldn't be discouraged if there are still remnants of pain after finishing therapy for a few weeks.

Other Professional Help for Gaslighting Victims

Counseling is not the only help victims of gaslighting may need. In cases where a person has been severely traumatized, as is the case with narcissistic abuse, there are different measures one can take to maintain personal safety and well-being.

Hire an Attorney

This professional will advise you on various matters such as legalities, filing restraining orders, and more.

Hire a Private Investigator

In cases where you know your abuser is following or watching you, it can be helpful to have someone keeping an eye on them. This also helps in situations where the person stalking the victim has multiple phone numbers and aliases. Having a private investigator track them down can help you find out more about your abuser and what they are capable of.

Hire a Bodyguard

This may be helpful if the person stalking or harassing you is dangerous in some way. A professional bodyguard will have training on dealing with people who could pose a threat and keep you safe.

Hire a Car Service

If you feel like your safety is in danger and the person stalking or harassing you has access to your personal vehicle, it may be helpful to use a car service instead. This can help ensure that no one is following you home from work every day.

Use a Safe Cell Phone

It is important to have some form of communication with the outside world during this time. A new phone number can help keep you more protected from your abuser if they can track down your previous device and access all of its data/contacts. You may also consider purchasing another phone with a new number to keep your abuser from finding out any information about you.

Most people are probably not aware of the signs and symptoms associated with gaslighting. The good news is that it's never too late to get help with recovering from this complex form of abuse. Today, we hope you know more about what gaslighting is and how it can be treated. It's important to remember that while there may be no quick fix or simple solution, seeking professional assistance could make all the difference in your recovery process.

Conclusion

Gaslighting Recovery Workbook gave an in-depth analysis of the severity of emotional abuse. This book answered questions like: "What is emotional abuse? What is the meaning of gaslighting? How do we identify a gaslighter? And "Is it possible to heal from an abusive relationship?" It also discussed the consequences of a manipulative and abusive relationship on your life.

Part one of the book is centered on understanding the cunning nature of a gaslighter. It discusses the idea of emotional abuse and toxic behavior and sheds light on gaslighting in detail. It explores the meaning of the term gaslighting and ways of spotting a gaslighter. It helps you identify whether you are being gaslighted. *Gaslighting Recovery Workbook* also explores the behavior and traits of an abuser to give you a better idea of them.

This book also explained narcissists - who they are and how they are related to gaslighting. Narcissists are self-serving, insecure, and extremely manipulative individuals who will do anything to get things done their way. They do not care about anyone else and treat people as play objects. They use and abuse people for their own benefit. This book further detailed the grave consequences of manipulation and gaslighting that victims have to go through. The abused individuals are put through extreme mental and physical anguish that is not always visible.

Gaslighting Recovery Workbook provides strategies the victim can use to exit the toxic relationship. The book also recognizes the courage of victims of abuse that are finally able to pull themselves out of the abusive relationship as it can be a really tough situation to get out from. It is extremely difficult to escape the clutches of a narcissist- but it is not impossible. *Gaslighting Recovery Workbook* also discusses different ways through which you can heal yourself. It explained how the victim needs to take some time to understand that they have been gaslit and abused for so long. It also analyzes the importance of going over the relationship to see how things are exacerbated. This process is called the grieving process, and it is an extremely crucial part of healing. It helps you mourn the loss of your old self and the time lost.

Gaslighting Recovery Workbook then explored how the victim can regain their confidence and rebuild their self-esteem to move on. It stressed how important it is to work on your confidence after being gaslit for years. Abusers make you doubt your perception, your sense of reality, and your worth. It also discusses the importance of establishing boundaries and healing. It further discusses ways you can create strict boundaries, as developing them not only helps you maintain a safe distance from your abuser but also works wonders for your self-esteem. This book also discusses how important it is to form healthy relationships and how to form those relationships. It further discussed the importance of getting professional help.

Thank you for buying and reading/listening to our book. If you found this book useful/helpful please take a few minutes and leave a review on Amazon.com or Audible.com (if you bought the audio version).

References

a conscious rethink. (2016, August 25). 30 toxic traits that should have no place in your life. Aconsciousrethink.Com. https://www.aconsciousrethink.com/3865/30-toxic-behaviors-no-place-life/

Champion, L. (2020, August 26). 15 traits of toxic people to watch out for. Purewow.Com; PureWow. https://www.purewow.com/wellness/traits-of-toxic-people

Emotional and Psychological Abuse. (2017, January 26). Womenslaw.Org. https://www.womenslaw.org/about-abuse/forms-abuse/emotional-and-psychological-abuse

Gordon, S. (n.d.). What is emotional abuse? Verywellmind.Com. Retrieved from https://www.verywellmind.com/identify-and-cope-with-emotional-abuse-4156673

Kaitlyn Peabody, L. (2021, March 13). 12 types of emotional abuse that aren't physical violence. Thetherapygroup.Com; The Therapy Group. https://www.thetherapygroup.com/thetherapygroupblog/12-types-of-emotional-abuse-that-arent-physical-violence

What is emotional abuse? (n.d.). Reachout.Com. Retrieved from https://au.reachout.com/articles/what-is-emotional-abuse

(N.d.). Org.Uk. Retrieved from https://www.relate.org.uk/relationship-help/help-relationships/arguing-and-conflict/what-emotional-abuse

7 types of narcissists and what to look for. (2020, June 6). Betterhelp.Com; BetterHelp. https://www.betterhelp.com/advice/personality/7-types-of-narcissists-and-what-to-look-for/

A brief history of narcissism. (n.d.). Psychology Today. Retrieved from https://www.psychologytoday.com/us/blog/suffer-the-children/201906/brief-history-narcissism

Are you being gaslighted by a narcissist? (n.d.). Psychology Today. Retrieved from https://www.psychologytoday.com/intl/blog/women-autism-spectrum-disorder/202011/are-you-being-gaslighted-narcissist

Ettinger, E. (2021, November 9). Polyamory, polygamy, and more: What to know about non-monogamy. Health.Com; Health.com. https://www.health.com/relationships/polyamory-ethical-non-monogamy-polygamy

How to spot a narcissist. (n.d.). Psychology Today. Retrieved from https://www.psychologytoday.com/us/blog/toxic-relationships/201812/how-spot-narcissist

Kassel, G. (2019, January 30). 11 signs you're dating a narcissist — and how to deal with them. Healthline.Com. https://www.healthline.com/health/mental-health/am-i-dating-a-narcissist

Mann, J. (2021, April 28). The 7 types of narcissists you need to know about, according to a therapist. Instyle.Com; InStyle. https://www.instyle.com/lifestyle/hump-day/types-of-narcissists

Melinda. (n.d.). Narcissistic personality disorder - HelpGuide.Org. Retrieved from https://www.helpguide.org/articles/mental-disorders/narcissistic-personality-disorder.htm

Moore, A. (2020, April 27). There are at least 8 types of narcissists — which ones are dangerous? Mindbodygreen.Com; mindbodygreen. https://www.mindbodygreen.com/articles/types-of-narcissists

What is narcissism? (2021, July 22). Tikvahlake.Com. https://www.tikvahlake.com/blog/what-is-narcissism/

Who Was Narcissus? (n.d.). Psychology Today. Retrieved from https://www.psychologytoday.com/intl/blog/hide-and-seek/201803/who-was-narcissus

Womack, R. (2019, November 13). How gaslighting and narcissism are related. Regain.Us; ReGain. https://www.regain.us/advice/general/how-gaslighting-and-narcissism-are-related/

5 ways gaslighting attacks your sense of self. (n.d.). Psychology Today. Retrieved from https://www.psychologytoday.com/intl/blog/women-autism-spectrum-disorder/202006/5-ways-gaslighting-attacks-your-sense-self

Golani, Y. (2018). Is gaslighting emotional or mental abuse? Is it dangerous? - Thriveworks. https://thriveworks.com/blog/gaslighting-emotional-mental-abuse/

Mays, M. (2019, January 29). The Impact of Gaslighting. Partnerhope.Com. https://partnerhope.com/the-impact-of-gaslighting/

Nall, R., MSN, & CRNA. (2020, June 29). Gaslighting: What it is, long-term effects, and what to do. Medicalnewstoday.Com. https://www.medicalnewstoday.com/articles/long-term-effects-of-gaslighting

Psycom.Net - mental health treatment resource since 1996. (n.d.). Psycom.Net. Retrieved from https://www.psycom.net/gaslighting-what-is-it/

Silber, D. (2018). Gaslighting: Is it the ultimate form of betrayal? How does it affect the victims in the short and long-term? - Thriveworks. https://thriveworks.com/blog/gaslighting-ultimate-form-betrayal-short-long-term/

11 red flags of gaslighting in a relationship. (n.d.). Psychology Today. Retrieved from https://www.psychologytoday.com/us/blog/here-there-and-everywhere/201701/11-red-flags-gaslighting-in-relationship

Am I being gaslighted? 15 relationship red flags to be aware of. (n.d.). Hellorelish.Com. Retrieved from https://hellorelish.com/articles/gaslighting-in-a-relationship.html

Ashley Laderer, S. R. (2021, July 23). How to spot gaslighting: 6 things that gaslighters say to manipulate you. Insider.Com; Insider. https://www.insider.com/gaslighting-examples

Baker, J. (2018, March 1). When abusive relationships end: a complex grief. Org.Uk; Counselling Directory. https://www.counselling-directory.org.uk/memberarticles/when-abusive-relationships-end-a-complex-grief

Concannon, C. (2020, November 22). How to recover after a toxic relationship - EVOKE. Evoke.Ie. https://evoke.ie/2020/11/22/life-style/how-to-recover-after-a-toxic-relationship

Gaslighting: How to Recognize it and What to Say When it Happens. (2020, July 7). Thepsychologygroup.Com. https://thepsychologygroup.com/gaslighting-how-to-recognize-it-and-what-to-say-when-it-happens/

Gattuso, R. (2019, November 22). How to spot — and heal from — gaslighting. Talkspace.Com. https://www.talkspace.com/blog/gaslighting-in-relationships-signs-how-to-spot/?__cf_chl_captcha_tk__=oed038GkN1DEcW7dun7u3UldHMKjDpTiaLOrqBa5NgA-1636689422-0-gaNycGzNDL0

Gordon, S. (n.d.). What Is Gaslighting? Verywellmind.Com. Retrieved from https://www.verywellmind.com/is-someone-gaslighting-you-4147470

Rogers, T., & Verasammy, K.-J. (2017, May 20). Healing the heart after a toxic relationship — Wholeness and Wellness Counselling Services. Wholenessandwellnesscounselling.Com; Wholeness and Wellness Counselling Services. http://wholenessandwellnesscounselling.com/blog-counselling-in-trinidad-and-tobago/2017/5/20/healing-the-heart-after-a-toxic-relationship

Stern, R. (2018, December 19). I've counseled hundreds of victims of gaslighting. Here's how to spot if you're being gaslighted. Vox. https://www.vox.com/first-person/2018/12/19/18140830/gaslighting-relationships-politics-explained

What it's like to grieve an abusive relationship. (2018, December 6). Themighty.Com. https://themighty.com/2018/12/grieving-miss-abusive-relationship/

(N.d.). Modernintimacy.Com. Retrieved from https://www.modernintimacy.com/13-tips-for-how-to-heal-from-a-toxic-relationship/

6 unexpected ways I've healed from gaslighting abuse and learned to trust myself again - everyday feminism. (2016, March 28). Everydayfeminism.Com. https://everydayfeminism.com/2016/03/healed-from-gaslighting-abuse/

Andersen, C. H. (2020, November 17). 16 gaslighting phrases that are red flags. Thehealthy.Com. https://www.thehealthy.com/family/relationships/gaslighting-phrases/

Bennett, T. (2018). What are gaslighting techniques? These master manipulators undermine, contradict, and disorient their victims - Thriveworks. https://thriveworks.com/blog/gaslighting-techniques-manipulators-undermine-contradict-victims/

Moore, A. (2020, November 16). "you're too sensitive" & other common phrases used by gaslighting parents. Mindbodygreen.Com; mindbodygreen. https://www.mindbodygreen.com/articles/signs-of-gaslighting-parents

Rebuilding after a gaslighting or narcissistic relationship. (n.d.). Psychology Today. Retrieved from https://www.psychologytoday.com/us/blog/here-there-and-everywhere/201907/rebuilding-after-gaslighting-or-narcissistic-relationship

Sarkis, S. (2021, March 12). How to regain your sanity after you've been gaslighted. Mindbodygreen.Com; mindbodygreen. https://www.mindbodygreen.com/articles/what-to-do-when-youve-been-gaslighted

Stern, R. (2018, December 19). I've counseled hundreds of victims of gaslighting. Here's how to spot if you're being gaslighted. Vox. https://www.vox.com/first-person/2018/12/19/18140830/gaslighting-relationships-politics-explained

8 ways to deal with gaslighting. (2021, September 9). Healthline.Com. https://www.healthline.com/health/how-to-deal-with-gaslighting

gwynn. (2017, February 14). Gaslighting & Boundaries. Gwynnraimondi.Com. https://gwynnraimondi.com/gaslighting-boundaries/

Ifeoluwa. (2019, October 23). 6 ways to deal with gaslighting. Stylecommodity.Com. http://www.stylecommodity.com/how-to-deal-with-gaslighting/

Infinum Growth Insights. (2018, December 30). Gaslighting Relationships - Setting boundaries to protect oneself. Infinumgrowth.Com. https://www.infinumgrowth.com/gaslighting-relationships-setting-boundaries/

Jennifer Liles MSW, L. (2019, May 30). On boundaries: 13 ways gaslighting crosses boundaries. Oomm.Live. https://www.oomm.live/13-ways-gaslighting-crosses-boundaries/

Johnson, E. B. (2020, December 3). What is gaslighting and how can you stop it? Practical Growth. https://medium.com/lady-vivra/what-is-gaslighting-and-how-to-stop-it-7560af4f2313

Mancao, A. "lia," & LCSW. (2021, April 16). What do you say when someone's gaslighting you? A therapist's go-to comebacks. Mindbodygreen.Com; mindbodygreen. https://www.mindbodygreen.com/articles/how-to-deal-with-gaslighting

Pomerance, M. (2021, March 8). Why do boundaries make us feel bad? Thecandidly.Com; The Candidly. https://www.thecandidly.com/2019/why-does-setting-boundaries-make-us-feel-like-terrible-people

Soghomonian, I. (2019, September 23). Boundaries - Why are they important? Part 1 - The Resilience Centre. Com.Au. https://www.theresiliencecentre.com.au/boundaries-why-are-they-important/

8 ways to deal with gaslighting. (2021, September 9). Healthline.Com. https://www.healthline.com/health/how-to-deal-with-gaslighting

Lawler, M., & Laube, J. (n.d.). What is self-care and why is it critical for your health? Everydayhealth.Com. Retrieved from https://www.everydayhealth.com/self-care/

Rebuilding after a gaslighting or narcissistic relationship. (n.d.). Psychology Today. Retrieved from https://www.psychologytoday.com/us/blog/here-there-and-everywhere/201907/rebuilding-after-gaslighting-or-narcissistic-relationship

Sarkis, S. (2021, March 12). How to regain your sanity after you've been gaslighted. Mindbodygreen.Com; mindbodygreen. https://www.mindbodygreen.com/articles/what-to-do-when-youve-been-gaslighted

WHO | What do we mean by self-care? (2019). https://www.who.int/reproductivehealth/self-care-interventions/definitions/en/

13 proven ways to maintain a healthy relationship with Tony. (2021, January 12). Tonyrobbins.Com. https://www.tonyrobbins.com/ultimate-relationship-guide/healthy-relationship

-you-deserve/

Healthdirect Australia. (2021). Building and maintaining healthy relationships. https://www.healthdirect.gov.au/building-and-maintaining-healthy-relationships

Raypole, C. (2020, March 30). 9 tips, tools, and strategies for narcissistic abuse recovery. Healthline.Com. https://www.healthline.com/health/mental-health/9-tips-for-narcissistic-abuse-recovery

Usman. (2021, May 6). 7 tips for building a healthy relationship. Spunout.Ie. https://spunout.ie/sex-relationships/relationships/healthy-habits-new-relationships

(N.d.-a). Bridgestorecovery.Com. Retrieved from https://www.bridgestorecovery.com/blog/i-was-the-victim-of-gaslighting-how-treatment-helped-me-heal-after-a-nervous-breakdown/

(N.d.-b). Takechargeinc.Net. Retrieved from https://takechargeinc.net/individual-counseling-can-help-identify-and-deal-with-gaslighting/

(N.d.-c). Couplestherapyinc.Com. Retrieved from https://www.couplestherapyinc.com/narcissist-gaslighting/

(N.d.-d). Mindbodygreen.Com. Retrieved from https://www.mindbodygreen.com/articles/how-to-deal-with-gaslighting